VIOLENT CHILDREN

Other Books in the At Issue Series:

VIOLENT CHILDREN

Bryan J. Grapes, *Book Editor*

David Bender, *Publisher*
Bruno Leone, *Executive Editor*
Bonnie Szumski, *Editorial Director*
David M. Haugen, *Managing Editor*

AT ISSUE

An Opposing Viewpoints® Series

Greenhaven Press, Inc.
San Diego, California

Library of Congress Cataloging-in-Publication Data

Violent children / Bryan J. Grapes, book editor.
        p.   cm. — (At issue)
    Includes bibliographical references and index.
    ISBN 0-7377-0159-5 (lib. bdg. : alk. paper). —
ISBN 0-7377-0158-7 (pbk. : alk. paper)
    1. Children and violence. I. Grapes, Bryan J. II. Series: At issue
(San Diego, Calif.)
HQ784.V55V55   2000
303.6'083—dc21   99-30143
                                                                        CIP

©2000 by Greenhaven Press, Inc., PO Box 289009,
San Diego, CA 92198-9009

Printed in the U.S.A.

Table of Contents

Page

Introduction

On March 24, 1998, Mitchell Johnson and Andrew Golden arrived at Westside Middle School in Jonesboro, Arkansas, with an arsenal of high-powered firearms. Andrew pulled the school's fire alarm and the two boys waited for students and teachers to file out of the building before they opened fire. The boys killed four students and one teacher and wounded fifteen others. At the time of their arrests, Johnson was thirteen and Golden was eleven.

Compounding the horror of the events in Jonesboro is the fact that it is just another violent episode on a growing list of similar school shootings committed by children. On October 1, 1997, sixteen-year-old Luke Woodham killed two students in his Pearl, Mississippi, high school. On December 1, 1997, fourteen-year-old Michael Carneal killed three students and wounded eight others at Heath High School in West Paducah, Kentucky. And on May 21, 1998, fifteen-year-old Kipland Kinkel opened fire in a crowded cafeteria at Thurston High School in Springfield, Oregon, killing two students and wounding twenty-two others. Kinkel had murdered both his parents the previous night.

A generation out of control?

Many observers feel that these school shootings are part of a larger problem. According to Congressman Bill McCollum, "Violent juvenile crime is a national epidemic. Today's superpredators are feral, presocial beings with no sense of right and wrong." "For the past decade, juvenile felons have become younger and more vicious," declares Minnesota state representative Charlie Weaver. Authors James Alan Fox and Glenn Pierce argue that the "most significant change in the youth population has been in attitude. This new generation . . . is more inclined to resort to violence over trivial issues . . . or for no apparent reason." Fox and Pierce believe this is because many youths, particularly those in major urban centers, are "beset with idleness" and that a "growing number of teens . . . see few attractive alternatives to violence, drug use, and gang membership."

Other critics, however, feel that the juvenile crime rate has been exaggerated. Writer Annette Fuentes points out that "youth crime has not changed as dramatically as our perceptions of it." In the June 15, 1998, issue of the *Nation*, Fuentes cites a 1997 survey by the National Center for Juvenile Justice which found that "today's violent youth commits the same number of violent acts as his/her predecessor of 15 years ago." Fuentes feels that today's youth are the target of an anti-teen campaign being waged by politicians and the media, and that the shootings in Jonesboro and elsewhere are merely isolated incidents that have received a lion's share of media coverage. Fuentes contends that coverage of a small number of violent incidents, along with the views of politicians like

Congressman Bill McCollum, have fueled the public's erroneous perception that youth violence is out of control.

Nevertheless, other statistics indicate that America's children are becoming more violent. The National Center for Juvenile Justice studied juvenile crime trends from 1982 to 1992, and in 1995 released a report detailing an increase of 57 percent in the arrest rates for murder, forcible rape, and robbery among juveniles. The arrest rate for aggravated assault during that ten-year span went up 100 percent. Most disturbingly, the report predicts that the worst is yet to come. They projected an increase of 101 percent in the arrest rate for violent crime among children by 2010. In addition to proposing and passing legislation to stiffen the penalties for violent juvenile offenders, many lawmakers and social critics are asking: What causes children to become so cold-hearted and aggressive?

Pop culture

Much of the blame for the rise in violent crime among children has been laid on American popular culture. Many critics point out that children are steeped in media violence from a very early age. In this view, the constant bombardment of violent television programming, popular music, video games, and movies have desensitized children to the consequences of violent behavior. According to David Grossman,

> To have a child of three, four, or five watch a "splatter" movie, learning to relate to a character for the first 90 minutes and then in the last 30 minutes watch helplessly as that new friend is hunted and brutally murdered is the moral and psychological equivalent of introducing your child to a friend, letting her play with that friend, and then butchering that friend in front of your child's eyes. And this happens hundreds upon hundreds of times.

Gangsta rap has long been a popular target for pop culture critics. Many feel that performers like TuPac Shakur glorify violence and the street gang culture, and critics contend that rap groups encourage children to solve their problems with violence. "Few adults have any idea how violent and venomous some of these lyrics are," says Senator Sam Brownback. Brownback points to the connection between violent gangsta rap groups and the shooting in Jonesboro. Mitchell Johnson had become a fan of Tu-Pac Shakur and the group Bone Thugs ~N~ Harmony, and often quoted the violent lyrics. Johnson's mother and his teachers noticed that he became obsessed with street gang culture. He often flashed street gang hand signals in the school hallways and bragged to schoolmates that he belonged to a national gang called the Bloods. Mitchell himself has claimed that he may have been influenced by the music's violent themes.

Kids and guns

Some observers, however, believe that the causes of juvenile violence lie elsewhere. Robert E. Shepherd Jr. contends that the perceived rise in juvenile violence is partly due to the easy availability of guns. In 1997 Shepherd wrote, "While juveniles of even 15 years ago exhibited many of the same tendencies to confrontation and poor impulse control we see today, their access to firearms was much more limited. The bruises and cuts of a decade ago are more likely to be gunshot wounds today." He believes that much of the violent crime committed by juveniles today could be avoided if children did not have such easy access to guns. Studies indicate that most children who have carried a gun to school have obtained the weapon from their home. Several of the ten weapons used in the Jonesboro shooting belonged to Andrew Golden's grandfather, an Arkansas wildlife official. Both Andrew and Mitchell had been trained in the use of firearms and in hunting from a very early age. Investigators noted the chilling skill and accuracy that Johnson and Golden exhibited in the shooting spree: Of the thirty-six rounds the boys fired, they scored twenty-seven hits.

Dysfunctional families and juvenile violence

Some social critics contend that dysfunctional families influence aggressive behavior in children. According to counselor Tammy Bell, children who come from painful family situations tend to become vengeful. Bell points out that growing up in a household with little or no parental supervision tends to make a child "more negative, more angry, more disrespectful," and this seems to have been the case with Mitchell Johnson. Even before Mitchell's parents divorced in 1994, the Johnson house was a troubled one. Frequent visitors to the Johnson home report that the family lived in squalor. Mitchell regularly went long periods of time without parental supervision. His parents would occasionally lose track of him and the police would have to be called to track him down. Mitchell's situation did not improve much after his parents divorced. When Mitchell's mother moved to Arkansas she married Terry Woodard, an ex-convict with a history of drug and firearms violations.

Other experts argue that Bell's view is not entirely accurate. Psychologist Michael Schulman points out that many children who grew up in troubled homes do not go on to commit violent crimes, and that violent children can come from a variety of backgrounds, as the Jonesboro case illustrates. While Mitchell Johnson did come from a broken home and a troubled family background, Andrew Golden did not. By all accounts, the Goldens were a typical, hardworking American family. Andrew was raised in a financially stable, two-parent household and was showered with love and encouragement. Despite this background, he was a willing accomplice to Mitchell Johnson in the Jonesboro shootings.

Are the shootings in Jonesboro part of a larger trend in youth violence? The group most associated with juvenile violence in America are males aged 15 to 19. Several of the school shootings involved boys this age, although some were even younger. However, an even more ominous statistic is that by 2010 the male population between the ages of 15 and 19 will increase by 30 percent. This has led many social observers to predict that the United States is headed for a youth crime wave of unprecedented proportions. If this is indeed the case, then understanding why children are becoming more violent will be the first step toward reversing that trend. In *At Issue: Violent Children,* various commentators consider the root causes of violent behavior in young people.

1

Violent Song Lyrics Encourage Aggressive Behavior in Children

Debbie Pelley

Debbie Pelley is a teacher at Westside Middle School in Jonesboro, Arkansas. Mitchell Johnson, one of the two youths who have been convicted of killing four students and one teacher and wounding ten others on March 24, 1998, was a student in her English class. The following viewpoint is adapted from her testimony before the Senate Commerce Committee on June 16, 1998.

The message delivered by many of today's popular rap groups, like Bone Thugs ~N~ Harmony and TuPac Shakur, is that violence is an acceptable way of life. These groups in particular glamorize violence and the gangster lifestyle. Modern rap music may have been what inspired Mitchell Johnson to shoot 15 people at his school in Jonesboro, Arkansas, in March of 1998. Before Johnson started listening to rap he was a normal and respectful boy. When he started listening to TuPac Shakur, and others like him, he became obsessed with violence and gang culture.

M y name is Debbie Pelley. I am a teacher at Westside Middle School in Jonesboro, Arkansas and was present when four students and one teacher were killed and ten others injured by two 11- and 13-year-old boys as the students evacuated the school building when a false fire alarm sounded on March 24, 1998.

I was the English teacher for the 13-year-old, Mitchell Johnson, and had him in class an hour a day from August 15 to March 24. Mitchell was always respectful, using "yes ma'am" and "no ma'am" in his responses to me. In my class I never saw him exhibit anger, never saw him commit any hostile act toward any other student or exhibit any behavior that would make me think Mitchell could commit this act. In fact, he had a pleasant and even cheerful disposition and appeared to enjoy his many friends, and to enjoy life in general. In a discussion with 7th grade classes the first

Reprinted from "Labels and Lyrics: Do Parental Advisory Stickers Inform Consumers and Parents?" Debbie Pelley's testimony before the U.S. Senate Commerce Committee, June 16, 1998.

day they were back at school after this tragedy, a discussion led by myself and another licensed professional counselor, James N. Woods, students explored possible reasons Mitchell could have committed this act. The students said that Mitchell had been listening to gangster rap music, and in particular to TuPac Shakur. They also said he had started to change a lot in the last two or three months.

The negative influence of gangsta rap

On succeeding days numerous students on many occasions contributed the following information. TuPac Shakur and another rap group, Bone Thugs ~N~ Harmony, were Mitchell's favorite musical groups. (At this point I had never heard of either of these groups.) Mitchell brought this music to school with him; listened to it on the bus; tried listening to it in classes, sang the lyrics over and over at school, and played a cassette in the bathroom "about coming to school and killing all the kids." Students said that in the last couple of months Mitchell was always making the gang sign that is on the cover of TuPac's album, *All Eyez On Me*, and that Mitchell was far more into this music than anyone else they knew. Mitchell's mother, and Mitchell himself recently confirmed that he bought these albums this last Christmas, three months before the tragedy.

One boy brought a CD by TuPac that Mitchell had lent to him and told me I could keep it, saying he didn't want to have anything more to do with the music because he felt it may have been an influence in Mitchell's life that led to this tragedy.

These 12-year-old students showed me how to pull these lyrics by Tu-Pac and Bone Thugs off the internet (about 500 pages of violent lyrics) and then identified Mitchell's favorite albums and songs that he was always singing. Following are a few examples of titles and quotes from those songs the way they are recorded on the internet. I wish every adult would take the time to read these lyrics as I have done. Most adults would be in for quite a shock.

"Crept and We Came" by Bone Thugs from the album, *Eternal E. 1999:* "Cockin the 9 and ready to aim/Pullin the Trigger/To blow out your brains/Bone got a gang/Man we crept and we came." (This song has about 40 murder images like "putten them in the ground and pumpin the gun." Mitchell's mother recently confirmed that Mitchell is still very familiar with the lyrics to this song. The last words of this song are quite revealing considering the way Mitchell and Drew killed the five and injured the ten so stealthily.)

Several students verified that the theme and message of this music is that killing and being on death row are cool.

"Body Rott" by Bone Thugs from the album, *Art of War: World War I.* One refrain used over and over in this song is "Nigga the war shouldn't stop until these motherfucking cops' body rott, body rott." This song contains the "f" word 23 times and several references to bitches and hoes (their usual expressions for females).

"Life Goes On" from the *All Eyez On Me* album by TuPac: "My homie from high school/he's getting by/It's time to bury another brotha/ nobody cry."

"I Ain't Mad At Ya" by TuPac from the *All Eyez On Me* album: "I can see us after school/we'd bomb on the first motherfucker/With the wrong shit on."

"2 Of Amerikaz Most Wanted" by TuPac from the album *All Eyez On Me:* Some fitting words since they killed and injured all females but one are these two lines: "Picture perfect, I paint a perfect picture/bomb the hoochies with precision." Then the refrain "Ain't nuttin but a gangsta party" is repeated five times in the chorus, and the chorus is repeated several times in the song.

"Shorty Wanna Be A Thug" by TuPac from the *All Eyez On Me* album: "He was a nice middle class nigga/But nobody knew the evil he'd do when he got a little bigger/. . . Was only sixteen, yet convicted as a felon/With a bunch of old niggas." Chorus, "Say he wanna be/Shorties gonna be a Thug/Said he wanna be/One day he's gonna be/Said he's wanna be/Shorties gonna be's a thug." (Last part is repeated several times in each chorus.)

"Bury Me A G" by TuPac from the *Thug Life Vol. I* album: "I got nothen' to lose sos I choose to be a killer/Went from bangin' to slangin'/Now I'm a dope dealer/All my a payed tha price to be the boss/Back in school/Wrote tha rules on gettin' tossed/Popping rocks on the block was a past time/Pack a 9 all the time."

"Blaze It" by Bone Thugs from the album *The Art of War: World War II:* "I'm so high/If reefer really makes you happy, nigga blaze it/Hell yeah, Bell yeah/Stay smokin', chokin',/Rollin' blunts [blunts are big marijuana joints] and we love it/We smoke and choke/We smoke and choke, and we love it. (This is repeated several times.) "Now, I've been fucked up since the last weed song/and P.O.D.'d the whole night long."

The glamorization of violence

Several students verified that the theme and message of this music is that killing and being on death row are cool. The students themselves pointed out that the recording company that publishes TuPac is called Death Row Records and showed me that on the *All Eyez On Me* album the cover advertises upcoming Death Row releases and one of them is called *Death Row Compilation.* One of the songs by Bone Thugs ~N~ Harmony, "If I Could Teach the World" from the album *The Art Of War: World War I* says, "If I could teach the world, Then I would teach the world, whole wide world to be a thugsta just like me, like." That seems to be the point of their music.

On June 1, 1998 Mitchell Johnson's mother said that Mitchell himself said that the music may have influenced him and that the music sort of draws you in. She confirmed to me that Mitch did possess, and she still has, Mitchell's albums and cassettes by TuPac and by Bone Thugs. She knew he bought them this last Christmas before the shooting in March with money he had received as a Christmas present from relatives.

Mitchell told her he bought them himself and had no trouble purchasing them. As noted above, numerous students reported the first day back at school that Mitch had started to change a lot the last two or three months and was making gang signs in the hall and around school.

Mitch's mother said he had always loved music and had sung specials at church and school since he was very little and that he owned and sang western music and gospel music as well. She did not know Mitchell had any that had warning labels on it. (These warning labels are in very small print and barely legible.) When she questioned Mitchell recently, he said he was first exposed to rap music through a girl in the neighborhood in Minnesota who had TuPac's music. He said he liked it because it was different. That was two years ago, when Mitchell and the girl were both 11 years old.

Mitchell himself said that the music may have influenced him and that the music sort of draws you in.

Surveys in three middle schools in Arkansas and one in Missouri indicate that a large percentage of students in middle schools now listen to gangster rap music, ranging from 39% to 84% of students that listen to TuPac and from 37% to 84% that listen to Bone Thugs ~n~ Harmony. Surveys were conducted in three middle schools in Arkansas and one in Missouri. Following are the results [from the] schools in Arkansas:

- 1st school, 7th graders—39% like to listen to TuPac and 67% to Bone Thugs. 2nd school, 8th graders—68% like to listen to TuPac and 84% to Bone Thugs.
- 3rd school, 9th graders—82% like to listen to TuPac and 37% to Bone Thugs.

In a rural middle school in Missouri the survey was conducted in the 5th, 6th, 7th, and 8th grades. The results are as follows:

- 5th grade—65% to TuPac and 77% to Bone Thugs.
- 6th grade—65% to TuPac and 75% to Bone Thugs.
- 7th and 8th grades combined—58% to TuPac and 78% to Bone Thugs. (The teacher did not keep 7th and 8th grade results separate on these.)

Numerous students made comments on these surveys that they liked and listened to this music, but that their parents would not have a clue as to who these groups were. The warning labels are extremely small on these albums. I had to actually look for it to find it when the students told me this music had warning labels on it. All parents and teachers with whom I have talked are shocked as I was when they see the lyrics and when they learn how many students are listening to this music. One parent wept when she saw the lyrics to which her son was being exposed.

Children need to be protected from violent lyrics

I believe the message coming out of the tragedy in our school in Jonesboro, Arkansas is that even the good schools and responsible families can no longer protect their children from our society. Violent music is only one aspect of our culture but a very significant one that seems to have gotten very little attention in the recent school tragedies, and Bone Thugs and TuPac are only two of the many musical groups that are affecting our youth. According to the *Pittsburgh Post Gazette*, [on] May 22, 1998 Andrew Wurst, the 14-year-old boy who shot a teacher and injured two others in Edinboro, Pennsylvania, "called himself Satan and liked the rock group Marilyn Manson." (Marilyn Manson is a shock rocker known for his violent lyrics.)

I believe that legislators who are elected to represent and protect the citizens in our country should find a way to investigate the scope of this problem, to protect our children from this music, and to educate the parents and society even as I have been educated in the last several weeks.

For the lyrics to these songs above and about 55 more songs by Bone Thugs ~N~ Harmony with the same type of violence, gangs, profanity, sex, and drugs, go to http://henge.com/~msmith/Lyrics/el999/lyrics.html.

2

Violent Song Lyrics Do Not Encourage Aggressive Behavior in Children

Stephen Chapman

Stephen Chapman is a columnist and editorial writer for the Chicago Tribune *and his column appears in numerous newspapers across the country.*

Gangster rappers and shock rockers such as Marilyn Manson are unfairly blamed for the destructive behavior of some youths. Though much of the public has accepted it as fact, there has been no study that has proven that violent music inspires violent behavior, or that entertainment influences behavior at all. Babyboomers were raised on wholesome entertainers such as Connie Francis, yet they ushered in the drug culture of the 1960s. Many adults read crime novels and horror stories without resorting to the violent behavior contained in them. Adults, as well as children, are capable of listening to music that contains violent themes without becoming violent themselves.

Recently, noting that Elton John's "Candle in the Wind" was the No. 1 single on the Billboard charts, that LeAnn Rimes' *You Light Up My Life* was the No. 2 album, and that Celine Dion continues to rack up sales by the truckload, a Senate subcommittee convened a hearing to debate whether American popular music is becoming unbearably saccharine.

Not really. Actually, the subcommittee was concerned about the existence of rock and rap music recordings that "glorify violence, murder and mayhem and condone the abuse of women," in the words of chairman Sam Brownback, R-Kan. "We as a society have grown coarser, meaner and more alienated," and Brownback thinks one reason is the prevalence of disagreeable messages in much of the music young people listen to.

As proof, the committee heard testimony from Raymond Kuntz, a North Dakota man whose 15-year-old son killed himself. The father blamed the tragedy on the boy's preoccupation with shock rocker Marilyn Manson, whose songs could be interpreted as glorifying suicide. Brownback said that over the past 30 years, teen suicide has tripled and violent crime by juveniles has risen sixfold, implying that diabolical music is at least partly to blame.

To their credit, the senators disavowed any interest in legislating against the problem, insisting that they were merely trying to encourage the recording industry to behave more responsibly.

But some senators expressed impatience with the view that the First Amendment is the last word on censorship. And being investigated by Congress is intimidating nonetheless: Anyone who declines to take "voluntary" action knows that mandatory measures may always be invoked.

Unfortunately, the debate on popular music lyrics never seems to go anywhere. Critics cite disgusting passages from this song or degrading images from that video. Musicians and free-speech defenders raise the banner of artistic truth and constitutional rights. Then, a year or two later, we go through the same exercise all over again. Somehow, we always pass over the important question of whether they do any real harm.

Brownback, noting the increase in teen suicide and violence, thinks there is no doubt. But the trend, by his own admission, began about the time the Monkees and Tommy James were the rage, long before the rise of bizarre rockers and potty-mouthed rappers.

Although popular wisdom takes it for granted that gore and vulgarity promote anti-social behavior, the evidence for that proposition is maddeningly elusive.

Lately, things have been improving, despite all the vile music Brownback deplores. Adolescent crime rates have been falling for five years. Among those between the ages of 15 and 19, suicide rose by 28 percent between 1980 and 1992. Among those aged 20 to 24, however, it dropped by 7 percent. It makes no more sense to blame rock and rap for the increase among teen-agers than it does to give them credit for the decline among young adults.

Although popular wisdom takes it for granted that gore and vulgarity promote anti-social behavior, the evidence for that proposition is maddeningly elusive. Baby boomers were raised on Connie Francis, Hayley Mills and *Father Knows Best*, but they ended up dropping acid, spurning authority, reveling in the sexual revolution and producing the biggest crime wave of the century. Wholesome entertainment doesn't necessarily produce wholesome behavior.

Nor does raunchy, violent fare lead inexorably to dangerous, irresponsible conduct. Millions of adults read real-crime books, murder mysteries and vampire novels without feeling the slightest urge to spill blood. They are acting on an ageless desire to inspect and even enjoy the dark and unfamiliar elements of human nature at a safe distance.

So are most kids who listen to the music decried by senators. Plenty of affluent white teen-agers buy CDs by thug rappers, but they don't really want to get a pistol and shoot cops. They merely want a window onto a subculture that is very different from their own.

The fans of death metal groups are likewise exploring something they find fascinating without necessarily wanting to imitate it. To believe that Marilyn Manson could talk a kid into suicide is to greatly exaggerate the power of music. Censors from time immemorial have made the mistake of assuming that human beings are helpless before the power of words and images, instead of recognizing that we respond to them as rational agents, capable of taming them for our own purposes. In 20 years, you can bet, the overwhelming majority of the people listening to shock rock and gangsta rap today will be law-abiding, tax-paying, mortgage-holding citizens with families and jobs. And you know what else? They'll be worried about what their kids are listening to.

3

Television Contributes to Violent Behavior in Children

Joanne Cantor

Joanne Cantor is a professor of communication arts at the University of Wisconsin-Madison. She is the author of Mommy, I'm Scared. *The focus of her book and her research has been the effects of mass media on children. This viewpoint is adapted from testimony Cantor gave before the House Subcommittee on Early Childhood, Youth and Families on April 8, 1998.*

There is overwhelming evidence that the viewing of violent programs on television contributes to violent behavior in children. The media glorifies and trivializes violence and sends the message to young people that violence is an acceptable way to solve problems. Children are much more susceptible to violent programming because they have not yet developed the ability to distinguish between fantasy and reality. Prolonged exposure to violent television programming desensitizes children to the consequences of violence. A more thorough ratings system is needed to ensure that parents will be able to screen out television's harmful effects.

M r. Chairman and members of the Subcommittee, I am pleased to appear before you to present my views on the causes of violence in children. For the past 23 years, I have been a professor at the University of Wisconsin, focusing my teaching and research on the effects of the mass media on children. Recently, I have participated in the National Television Violence Study, research that explores the television landscape and the harm done to children by exposure to television violence. I have a book due out in September 1998, titled *Mommy, I'm Scared,* which helps parents protect their children from the effects of media violence. Finally, and not the least important, I am the mother of a nine-year-old son, so I can address these issues as a parent as well as a researcher and author.

As you will hear today, there are many factors that contribute to chil-

Reprinted from Joanne Cantor's testimony before the U.S. House of Representatives Committee on Education and the Workforce, Subcommittee on Early Childhood, Youth, and Families, April 8, 1998.

dren behaving violently. Having done research on this issue myself, and having reviewed the vast and growing literature on this topic, I can say without hesitation that media violence is a substantial contributor to our children becoming violent, becoming desensitized to the consequences of violence, and becoming fearful of being a victim. Media images of violence make their contributions both in the short-term, immediately after viewing, and in the long-term as a cumulative effect of repeated exposure to violent images throughout childhood. There is an overwhelming consensus on this point among researchers and among public health organizations. Our youngest children are the most vulnerable, both because they are in the process of forming their own sense of right and wrong, and because they are not yet adept at distinguishing fantasy from reality. A recent meta-analysis of more than 200 studies involving more than 1,000 comparisons showed that viewing violence in programs of a wide range of types consistently contributes to a wide array of violent behaviors ranging from stated intentions to commit violence to actual criminal violence.

How violence is portrayed

Research shows that the way violence is portrayed can make it more or less likely that a child will adopt violent attitudes or become violent. For example, violence that is committed by "good guys," that is shown as justified, and that shows little visible pain or harm is more likely to be imitated than violence committed by evil characters or violence that brings pain or punishment. The National Television Violence Study, which recently released its Year Three report on the most representative and extensive sample of television programs ever studied, showed that not only has violence remained at a high level on television (3 out of every 5 programs contain violence), the way most violence is portrayed is destined to promote children's aggression. For example, in more than 40% of programs with violence, the "bad" violent characters are never punished; and only 4% of violent programs portray a theme that promotes nonviolence. Moreover, more than half of the violent interactions on television show no pain, and almost 40% of violent interactions show good guys behaving violently. If someone set out to design an ad campaign to promote violence by making it seem glamorous, effective, risk-free, and painless, they could hardly do better if they tried.

> *I can say without hesitation that media violence is a substantial contributor to our children becoming violent.*

When we see children commit unspeakable and unexplainable acts of violence, it is natural to ask whether repeated exposure to media violence that is glamorized, sanitized, and trivialized contributed to their behavior. There is no doubt that each tragedy is the result of many unhealthy influences working together. But when a child resorts to gunfire to correct what he sees as an injustice, is it unreasonable to think that repeated exposure to violent incidents on television—25% of which involve guns

—might have provided encouragement to act that way? In many of these well-publicized incidents, the young perpetrators seem surprised at the severity of the consequences to themselves and their victims. Maybe the fact that violence on television usually underplays violence's negative effects has something to do with this.

Although television violence is not the strongest contributor to children's violent behavior, it is the one over which we may have the most control. Producers and distributors of television programs make choices of what to show, and it is in their power to provide programming that is more or less likely to produce harm.

What else can we do besides urging the media to be more responsible?

Television distorts reality

We need better parent education about the effects of media violence on children. When parents understand the harmful effects, they will be motivated to act in protective ways. We also need to promote media literacy education for children. Teaching children about the effects of television and teaching them the ways in which television distorts the reality of violence can help reduce many of the negative effects of what they see.

Speaking personally as a parent who has a TV, a major problem is that TV automatically makes available in my home thousands of programs I would never select if I were making the choice. Rather than having the option of selecting what I want my child to see, everything is accessible at the touch of a remote, and I only have the option of playing defense—actively working to shield my child from what I consider the worst of it. Given that I must play defense, I need accurate information about the content of programs. TV ratings can help but only if all stations (including NBC)[1] use ratings that at least point to where the violence is: and the ratings will need to be assigned accurately and consistently. Blocking technologies like the V-chip, that will permit parents to keep the most harmful programs from entering our homes, will need to be effective and user-friendly.

If all of us want to help parents socialize their children well, it will be important that research be continued to monitor the TV landscape and to keep tabs on how appropriately television programs are being rated, whether the existing rating system needs to be modified further and how well the V-chip and other blocking devices are working. We need to ensure that these new tools really help parents reduce TV's negative influences and help promote children's healthy development. In spite of the enormity and complexity of the problem of child violence and the fact that aggression-promoting images seem firmly entrenched in the television landscape, I believe that media education for parents and children, better labeling of programs, and effective blocking tools can really make a difference.

Notes

1. NBC refuses to go along with the amended TV rating system, implemented in October, 1997, which adds content letters, including a V for violence, to the original age-based TV Parental Guidelines. The Year Three re-

search of the National Television Violence Study showed that without the content letters, the age-based ratings of TVG, TVPG, TV 14, and TVMA are unrelated to the presence of violence in programs.

References

Cantor, J. (1998). Forthcoming. *Mommy, I'm Scared: How TV and Movies Frighten Children and What We Can Do to Protect Them.* San Diego: Harvest Books/Harcourt Brace.

Federman, J. (Ed. 1998). Executive Summary National Television Violence Study, Volume 3. Santa Barbara, CA: Center for Communication and Social Policy, University of California, Santa Barbara.

National Television Violence Study (Volumes 1, 2, and 3, 1996. 1997, and 1998, respectively). Thousand Oaks. CA: Sage Publications.

Paik, H., & Comstock, G. (1994). *The Effects of Television Violence on Antisocial Behavior: A Meta-analysis.* Communication Research, 21(4), 516–539.

4

Television Does Not Contribute to Violent Behavior in Children

Mike Males

Mike Males is a social-ecology doctoral student at the University of California, Irvine, and the author of The Scapegoat Generation: America's War on Adolescents.

Children are not as easily influenced by television and mass media as some think. If a youth is exhibiting destructive behavior, he or she has most likely learned it from the adults in his or her life. Violence is one of many negative behaviors, including binge drinking and drug abuse, that children learn from their parents or other adults in their lives, not from the media. Studies that indicate children learn violent behavior by watching television have no basis in fact and are part of an anti-youth campaign being waged by conservative and progressive alike.

"Children have never been very good at listening to their elders," James Baldwin wrote in *Nobody Knows My Name*. "But they have never failed to imitate them." This basic truth has all but disappeared as the public increasingly treats teenagers as a robot-like population under sway of an exploitative media. White House officials lecture film, music, Internet, fashion, and pop-culture moguls and accuse them of programming kids to smoke, drink, shoot up, have sex, and kill.

So do conservatives, led by William Bennett and Dan Quayle. Professional organizations are also into media-bashing. In its famous report on youth risks, the Carnegie Corporation devoted a full chapter to media influences.

Progressives are no exception. *Mother Jones* claims it has "proof that TV makes kids violent." And the Institute for Alternative Media emphasizes, "the average American child will witness . . . 200,000 acts of [TV] violence" by the time that child graduates from high school.

None of these varied interests note that during the eighteen years be-

Reprinted from Mike Males, "Who Us? Stop Blaming Kids and TV (for Crime and Substance Abuse)," *The Progressive*, October 1, 1997, by permission of *The Progressive*, 409 E. Main St., Madison, WI 53703.

tween a child's birth and graduation from high school, there will be fifteen million cases of real violence in American homes grave enough to require hospital emergency treatment. These assaults will cause ten million serious injuries and 40,000 deaths to children. In October 1996, the Department of Health and Human Services reported 565,000 serious injuries that abusive parents inflicted on children and youths in 1993. The number is up four-fold since 1986.

The Department of Health report disappeared from the news in one day. It elicited virtually no comment from the White House, Republicans, or law-enforcement officials. Nor from Carnegie scholars, whose 150-page study, "Great Transitions: Preparing Adolescents for a New Century," devotes two sentences to household violence. The left press took no particular interest in the story, either.

All sides seem to agree that fictional violence, sex on the screen, Joe Camel, beer-drinking frogs, or naked bodies on the Internet pose a bigger threat to children than do actual beatings, rape, or parental addictions. This, in turn, upholds the Clinton doctrine that youth behavior is the problem, and curbing young people's rights the answer.

Misleading claims

Claims that TV causes violence bear little relation to real behavior. Japanese and European kids behold media as graphically brutal as that which appears on American screens, but seventeen-year-olds in those countries commit murder at rates lower than those of American seventy-year-olds.

Likewise, youths in different parts of the United States are exposed to the same media but display drastically different violence levels. TV violence does not account for the fact that the murder rate among black teens in Washington, D.C., is twenty-five times higher than that of white teens living a few Metro stops away. It doesn't explain why, nationally, murder doubled among nonwhite and Latino youth over the last decade, but declined among white Anglo teens. Furthermore, contrary to the TV brainwashing theory, Anglo sixteen-year-olds have lower violent-crime rates than black sixty-year-olds, Latino forty-year-olds, and Anglo thirty-year-olds. Men, women, whites, Latinos, blacks, Asians, teens, young adults, middle-agers, and senior citizens in Fresno County—California's poorest urban area—display murder and violent-crime rates double those of their counterparts in Ventura County, the state's richest.

Confounding every theory, America's biggest explosion in felony violent crime is not street crime among minorities or teens of any color, but domestic violence among aging, mostly white baby boomers. Should we arm Junior with a V-chip to protect him from Mom and Dad?

In practical terms, media-violence theories are not about kids, but about race and class: If TV accounts for any meaningful fraction of murder levels among poorer, nonwhite youth, why doesn't it have the same effect on white kids? Are minorities inherently programmable?

The newest target is Channel One, legitimately criticized by the Unplug Campaign—a watchdog sponsored by the Center for Commercial-Free Public Education—as a corporate marketing ploy packaged as educational TV. But then the Unplug Campaign gives credence to claims that "commercials control kids" by "harvesting minds," as Roy Fox of the University of Missouri says. These claims imply that teens are uniquely open to media brainwashing.

Other misleading claims come from Johns Hopkins University media analyst Mark Crispin Miller. In his critique of Channel One in the May 1997 edition of *Extra!*, Miller invoked such hackneyed phrases as the "inevitable rebelliousness of adolescent boys," the "hormones raging," and the "defiant boorish behavior" of "young men." Despite the popularity of these stereotypes, there is no basis in fact for such anti-youth bias.

Claims that TV causes violence bear little relation to real behavior.

A 1988 study in the *Journal of Youth and Adolescence* by psychology professors Grayson Holmbeck and John Hill concluded: "Adolescents are not in turmoil, not deeply disturbed, not at the mercy of their impulses, not resistant to parental values, and not rebellious."

In the November 1992 *Journal of the American Academy of Child and Adolescent Psychiatry*, Northwestern University psychiatry professor Daniel Offer reviewed 150 studies and concluded, in his article "Debunking the Myths of Adolescence," that "the effects of pubertal hormones are neither potent nor pervasive."

If anything, Channel One and other mainstream media reinforce young people's conformity to—not defiance of—adult values. Miller's unsubstantiated claims that student consumerism, bad behaviors, and mental or biological imbalances are compelled by media ads and images could be made with equal force about the behaviors of his own age group. Binge drinking, drug abuse, and violence against children by adults over the age of thirty are rising rapidly.

The barrage of sexually seductive liquor ads, fashion images, and anti-youth rhetoric, by conventional logic, must be influencing those hormonally unstable middle-agers.

Cross generational problems

I worked for a dozen years in youth programs in Montana and California. When problems arose, they usually crossed generations. I saw violent kids with dads or uncles in jail for assault. I saw middle-schoolers molested in childhood by mom's boyfriend. I saw budding teen alcoholics hoisting forty-ouncers alongside forty-year-old sots. I also saw again and again how kids start to smoke. In countless trailers and small apartments dense with blue haze, children roamed the rugs as grownups puffed. Mom and seventh-grade daughter swapped Dorals while bemoaning the evils of men. A junior-high basketball center slept outside before a big game because a dozen elders—from her non-inhaling sixteen-year-old brother to her grandma—were all chain smokers. Two years later, she'd given up and joined the party.

As a rule, teen smoking mimicked adult smoking by gender, race, locale, era, and household. I could discern no pop-culture puppetry. My survey of 400 Los Angeles middle schoolers for a 1994 *Journal of School Health* article found children of smoking parents three times more likely to smoke by age fifteen than children of nonsmokers. Parents were the most influential but not the only adults kids emulated. Nor did youngsters copy elders slavishly. Youths often picked slightly different habits (like chewing tobacco, or their own brands).

In 1989, the Centers for Disease Control lamented, "75 percent of all teenage smokers come from homes where parents smoke." You don't hear such candor from today's put-politics-first health agencies. Centers for Disease Control tobacco chieftain Michael Eriksen informed me that his agency doesn't make an issue of parental smoking. Nor do anti-smoking groups. Asked Kathy Mulvey, research director of INFACT: "Why make enemies of fifty million adult smokers" when advertising creates the real "appeal of tobacco to youth?"

Do ads hook kids on cigarettes? Studies of the effects of the Joe Camel logo show only that a larger fraction of teen smokers than veteran adult smokers choose the Camel brand. When asked, some researchers admit they cannot demonstrate that advertising causes kids to smoke who would not otherwise. And that's the real issue. In fact, surveys found smoking declining among teens (especially the youngest) during Joe's advent from 1985 to 1990.

The University of California's Stanton Glantz, whose exposure of 10,000 tobacco documents enraged the industry, found corporate perfidy far shrewder than camels and cowboys.

"As the tobacco industry knows well," Glantz reported, "kids want to be like adults." An industry marketing document advises: "To reach young smokers, present the cigarette as one of the initiations into adult life . . . the basic symbols of growing up."

Kids imitate adults

The biggest predictor of whether a teen will become a smoker, a drunk, or a druggie is whether or not the child grows up amid adult addicts. Three-fourths of murdered kids are killed by adults. Suicide and murder rates among white teenagers resemble those of white adults, and suicide and murder rates among black teens track those of black adults. And as far as teen pregnancy goes, for minor mothers, four-fifths of the fathers are adults over eighteen, and half are adults over twenty.

The inescapable conclusion is this: If you want to change juvenile behavior, change adult behavior. But instead of focusing on adults, almost everyone points a finger at kids—and at the TV culture that supposedly addicts them.

Groups like Mothers Against Drunk Driving charge, for instance, that Budweiser's frogs entice teens to drink. Yet the 1995 National Household Survey found teen alcohol use declining. "Youths aren't buying the cute and flashy beer images," an in-depth *USA Today* survey found. Most teens found the ads amusing, but they did not consume Bud as a result.

By squabbling over frogs, political interests can sidestep the impolitic tragedy that adults over the age of twenty-one cause 90 percent of America's 16,000 alcohol-related traffic deaths every year. Clinton and drug-policy chief Barry McCaffrey ignore federal reports that show a skyrocketing toll of booze- and drug-related casualties among adults in their thirties and forties—the age group that is parenting most American teens. But both officials get favorable press attention by blaming alcohol ads and heroin chic for corrupting our kids.

Adolescents are not in turmoil, not deeply disturbed, not at the mercy of their impulses, not resistant to parental values, and not rebellious.

Progressive reformers who insist kids are so malleable that beer frogs and Joe Camel and Ace Ventura push them to evil are not so different from those on the Christian right who claim that *Our Bodies, Ourselves* promotes teen sex and that the group Rage Against the Machine persuades pubescents to roll down Rodeo Drive with a shotgun.

America's increasingly marginalized young deserve better than grownup escapism. Millions of children and teenagers face real destitution, drug abuse, and violence in their homes. Yet these profound menaces continue to lurk in the background, even as the frogs, V-chips, and Mighty Morphins take center stage.

5

Video Games Cause Aggressive Behavior in Children

Stephen Barr

Stephen Barr is a contributor to Reader's Digest *magazine.*

Modern video games are becoming more realistic in their depictions of graphic violence. Children who play these games are regularly taking an active part in decapitations, bodily dismemberment, and other grisly acts without encountering any of the real-life consequences of committing such actions. The current video game rating system is inadequate and it does not ensure that games with mature themes will not fall into the hands of young, impressionable children. Each time a child plays a violent video game he or she is being conditioned to accept brutality as a way of life.

Dinner was almost ready when the killing occurred. Don Wise wandered into the living room of his home in Leawood, Kansas, one evening last September. His ten-year-old son, Mike, and a 12-year-old friend were sitting in front of a large-screen television set. They were playing a video game they had rented called Goldeneye 007, one of the top-selling titles of 1998.

Standing behind the boys, Wise saw that the video, rated T (Teen) for ages 13 and older, depicted the shooter's point of view, with his large gun jutting into the bottom of the TV frame. After a few minutes Mike's friend cornered an unarmed opponent and held the gun to his head at point-blank range. "You can't get away!" the boy said with a maniacal sneer, taunting the character on the screen. "You're mine!"

The boy pushed the button and shot the character in the face. Blood splattered the lab coat of the character as he whirled and fell. "You're down!" the boy said, laughing.

Chilled by the child's obvious glee, Wise ordered the boys to turn the game off. "This game is disgusting," he said sternly. "I don't want you to play with this anymore."

Reprinted, with permission, from Stephen Barr, "Computer Violence: Are Your Kids at Risk?" *Reader's Digest*, January 1999.

Explains Wise, "I'm not going to invite somebody into my house to teach kids to kill."

Murder and mayhem

Video games have become a pervasive form of entertainment in the 1990s. Today an estimated 69 percent of American families own or rent video and computer games. Most are harmless entertainment, but in far too many of the most popular ones, kids are acting out realistic violent experiences on their TV and computer screens. They are severing heads and snapping spines in Mortal Kombat IV. They are paying a go-go dancer to flash her breasts and then blowing her away in Duke Nukem 3D. They are scorching the high school band with a flamethrower until they burn to death in Postal.

We're teaching kids in the most incredible manner what it's like to pull the trigger.

"These are not just games anymore," says Rick Dyer, president of the San Diego–based Virtual Image Productions and an outspoken critic of titles with violent and sexual content. "These are learning machines. We're teaching kids in the most incredible manner what it's like to pull the trigger. The focus is on the thrill, enjoyment and reward. What they're *not* learning are the real-life consequences."

Interactive video games introduce kids to a fantasy world that features amazingly lifelike characters, detailed images of brutality, and an audio mix of heart-pounding music, macabre sound effects and authentic voices. Unlike movies and television, where you watch the violence, the game lets you feel the sensation of committing violent acts. When you're into the game, you're *in* the game.

"The technology is becoming more engaging for kids," says David Walsh, president of the National Institute on Media and the Family (NIMF), a watchdog group in Minneapolis, "and a segment of games features antisocial themes of violence, sex and crude language. Unfortunately, it's a segment that seems particularly popular with kids ages eight to 15."

Action games

With the rapid evolution of game technology comes a generation of titles portraying three-dimensional, 360-degree environments that are virtually real. "We are moving very close to a real cinematic experience, pushing the boundaries of what a TV set or computer monitor can deliver," says Steve Grossman, chairman and CEO of ASC Games. "In the next five years there will be nothing you cannot portray."

Grossman makes no apologies for the uptick in blood and gore, saying these features are a way to "get people to talk about the game." In Grand Theft Auto, a 1998 ASC release, kids get to assume the role of a low-level mobster and perform various murders and other felonies to impress their boss. Because of the cartoonlike design, Grossman insists the game is a spoof. "If anyone takes Grand Theft Auto seriously," he says, "they have a real problem separating fantasy from reality." (The game has been taken seriously by officials in France and Great Britain, who have condemned it; the Brazilian government has banned it.)

During Christmas 1997, Postal was another title that generated controversy. In that game kids control a character known among players as The Postal Dude who "goes postal" when the bank forecloses on his house. On their rampage, players gun down anything that moves, including parishioners leaving a church. One victim wails, "My eyes! I can't see anything!" The Postal Dude occasionally mutters, "Only my gun understands me."

Makers of the more violent games are pushing the outer limits of savagery and depravity. One of the most hotly anticipated videos is the sequel to Carmageddon, in which the player racks up points for mowing down pedestrians. In Carmageddon 2: Carpocalypse Now, your victims not only squish under your tires and splatter blood on the windshield, they also get on their knees and beg for mercy, or commit suicide. If you like, you can also dismember them.

Immoral Kombat

In 1993 Sen. Joe Lieberman (D., Connecticut) and Sen. Herb Kohl (D., Wisconsin) held Congressional hearings on violent video games.

They successfully pressured the video-game industry to adopt a rating system to inform parents of games featuring violent and sexually oriented content. Started in 1994 by video-game developers, the Entertainment Software Rating Board (ESRB) divides games into five categories: EC for players in early childhood, E for everyone, T for teens 13 and older, M for mature players (17 and above) and AO for adults only. The rating appears on the front of every game box, while on the back are three or four words that describe the content.

In its four-year existence the ESRB has rated over 4000 titles, 70 percent of which are rated E. Parents can get ratings by contacting 800-771-ESRB or www.esrb.org. But the system is not designed to keep mature games away from children, says ESRB executive director Arthur I. Pober. "Our role is not to dictate taste," he explains. "We give parents the tools to determine what they do or don't want for their children."

Soldiers trained to kill in combat use the same brutalization and desensitization techniques now used to entertain children.

In 1996 the Minneapolis watchdog group NIMF developed a video game report card to help parents make informed choices about the games their kids played. (For NIMF ratings of games, contact www.mediaandthefamily.org and click on KidScore.) The latest annual report reflects the opinions of parents who evaluate the games based on violence, sexual content and language. Out of 90 titles reviewed, parents concluded that one-third, or 31 in all, deserved a more restrictive rating than the one given by the ESRB.

Asked about the discrepancy, the ESRB's Pober says that "every group will have a different mind-set. They're entitled to their views." He adds that the ESRB has not received any complaints that the "rating was inaccurate."

Easy access

As with the R rating on movies, youngsters are quite astute and know that an M rating on a video game means blood and gore. Moreover, they find they can easily obtain mature games, as long as they elude parental supervision.

There is no penalty for renting or selling M-rated titles to kids, and according to an NIMF survey, only 20 percent of stores have ratings policies that explain to cashiers which customers can and can't buy games.

With his father's permission, I enlisted the help of a ten-year-old boy to see if he could rent and buy M-rated video games. At Blockbuster Video, which has corporate policies about game rentals, it was a cinch for him to take out Mortal Kombat IV. At Supr Software, a video-game and software retailer, he bought Resident Evil II and Mortal Kombat IV, while at KB Toys he got Parasite Eve, a new release that contains, according to the box, mature sexual themes. "Yeah, sweet game," the cashier told the boy. "It's really cool."

Potential for harm

When it comes to the effects of video games on children, there's a double standard in the industry: While publishers trumpet educational games in helping develop kids' learning skills, they discount that violent games can have baser influences on behavior and attitudes. "There has been no evidence to show that video games increase violence in children," says Pat Becker of Electronic Arts, the industry's largest publisher.

Video-game developer Rick Dyer, whose company makes only E-rated titles, says the effects on children are "one of the dark secrets that this industry does not want to talk about, and for one reason: they're making money from it." It's the same kind of attitude that has allowed the tobacco industry to contend for so long that nicotine is not addictive. "There's no concern for the potential price we may pay in society," Dyer says. "It's strictly the dollar."

For decades the public has decried the increasing violence in Hollywood movies and on prime-time television. Researchers conclude there is a measurable increase of three to 15 percent in an individual's aggressive behavior after watching violent television.

"With a video game kids don't just observe an aggressor rewarded; they experience the direct reward," says Stanford communication professor Donald Roberts. "Engaging in these activities rather than watching them increases the potential for the negative effects to take hold."

Indeed, soldiers trained to kill in combat use the same brutalization and desensitization techniques now used to entertain children. Lt. Col. Dave Grossman of Jonesboro, Arkansas, a military expert on the psychology of killing, notes: "Every time a child plays a point-and-shoot video game, he is learning the exact same conditioned reflex skills as a soldier or police officer in training."

"The media are probably more powerful than we realize," says the NIMF's David Walsh. "And if parents are responsible for caring for their children, then our definition of *caring* has to keep pace with a changing media world."

6

Video Games Do Not Cause Aggressive Behavior in Children

Tom Kalinske

Tom Kalinske is the former president and CEO of Sega America, Inc., and now works for Educational Technology, LLC. This viewpoint is adapted from a speech that Kalinske gave before the Commonwealth Club of California on August 18, 1994.

Many parents fear video and computer games because their children have a more comprehensive understanding of the technology than they do. Those who argue that children will emulate the violent behavior in some video games are taking a very pessimistic view of kids. Every responsible study commissioned to examine the link between violence in video games and violent behavior in children has determined that children can differentiate between real violence and make-believe violence. Previous technological advances in entertainment, such as radio and movies, were also once blamed for destroying the moral well-being of children; video games are only the latest technology to be unfairly portrayed as encouraging destructive behavior in young people. Contrary to popular belief, video games help children to develop socially, and they help children to learn new technology that will be commonplace in tomorrow's job market.

Good afternoon, and thank you for this opportunity to talk about a subject which is both dear to my heart and extraordinarily important—the relationship between kids and technology—and why that relationship is so vital to their education and their future.

Let me begin with a story, a true story which originates from a friend of mine who was hired to shoot a documentary film about computers and education.

The film was about an experiment in a Southern California junior

Reprinted from Tom Kalinske, "Technology and Its Post-positive Impact on Kids," a speech delivered to the Commonwealth Club of California, San Francisco, August 18, 1994. Used by permission of the author.

high school, a test of a new computer system which was programmed with learning games that reinforced the fundamentals of math and reading and writing. This particular school was chosen to make the computer's job as tough as possible—because year after year, its students scored in the lowest statewide percentiles in every subject.

The experiment took place ten years ago, when computers were still pretty exotic contraptions to find in a public school. Naturally, the principal wanted to minimize the risk that the computers would be damaged in any way. And so he made a decision to exclude the special education class from the experiment.

You see, the special ed kids were always a bit out of control. It seemed you could never get them to pay much attention, and they'd fight at the drop of a hat. Their classroom was never really under control, and their academic performance—well, although these kids were technically in junior high school, few of them could read books or add numbers at much above a second grade level.

That would have been the end of the story if it weren't for a very dedicated special ed teacher. When she heard that her kids were going to sit on the sidelines while everyone else got time on the computers, she made such a fuss, that the principal gave in to this irresistible force.

And so, the special ed kids, whom the school system, and just about everyone else, had given up on, got their four hours a week at the computers. And when, in just one semester, some of these kids learned more than in the preceding ten years, the administration realized that something very special and very unexpected had happened.

There was an Hispanic girl in special ed because she just never learned to read. And she was terribly intimidated in class, so she never was able to communicate that she simply didn't get the basic phonic concepts. But the computer didn't intimidate her, and in one semester, she'd begun to read at her proper grade level.

The most touching story, however, was a kid named Raymond, who had every problem in the book. A dysfunctional home, acute shyness, bad eyesight and zero academic performance. But in the one semester he had with the computer, Raymond caught up seven years of math. They got him in front of the camera for an interview and asked how it was that he blossomed so magnificently.

"Well," he replied, "you see, all the kids here call me retard. The computer calls me Raymond."

The breakthrough for Raymond, and for many thousands of other kids who unlocked their academic potential with the help of technology, was a learning process based on exploration, discovery, constant feedback, and individual experience. Up until recently, the history of formal education has been a series of rejections of this learning model.

Technology and the job market

But these days, it's very clear that technology must play an increasingly important role preparing kids for a world where mastery of thinking machines is the key survival skill.

Just look how the job market has changed. A generation or two ago, a consumer products manufacturer the size of Sega would have had perhaps ten percent of its workforce designing products, half its workforce making them, and the rest handling administrative details. But today, we have over forty percent in R&D [research and development] and just 3 percent in traditional manufacturing. But in fact, it's the forty percent who are really making the games, the folks in the factory are just duplicating them. And most of the forty percent owe their jobs to the fact that they began playing with technology before they were ten years old.

Remember, it was just fifty years ago when Tom Watson, the founder of IBM, and usually a pretty reliable visionary, proclaimed that the world couldn't possibly need more than five computers. Today, the average Sega employee has 1.2 computers on his or her desk.

Video games help you to identify and belong, to earn the respect and admiration of kids who may be better athletes, or more socially polished, or can multiply six digit numbers together in their heads.

The pace of change has accelerated so rapidly that, for the first time, we parents are faced with the prospect of preparing our children for jobs most of us can't conceive of, and have frighteningly little to pass along in the way of experience. Fortunately, the kids have already started adapting.

Most children born after 1970 have a profoundly different relationship to technology than their parents. For most teachers and parents, technology may be useful, but it's usually intimidating. Who here hasn't complained about voice mail hell, inscrutable e-mail, unprogrammable VCRs, un-usable CD-ROMs.

But you've probably never heard a kid swear at a computer. Just watch a girl or boy walk up to an unfamiliar piece of software. It's like Vladimir Horowitz sitting down at an unfamiliar piano. There's no question about who's the master, and who's the slave.

Whether you're in the video game business, the education business, or the parenting business, it's vital to understand why kids have such an affinity for interactive software.

Let's frame the question this way . . . what's a kid's job description . . . what business are you in if you're 3 to 12 years old?

Well, you're probably in the business of figuring out how to understand and control the world around you. You have a short attention span, but a huge appetite for repetition, exaggeration, and sensory stimulation. You'd like pretending to be a warrior or a princess or a powerful magician, but your parents don't take you seriously. You've got really important things to accomplish, but you'd better accomplish them without slurping your soup at the dinner table.

The kid in command

Your parents love you, but they don't take you seriously enough. Not like interactive games. Here's a world where you're in total command—you can open every door, push every button, run as fast as you please, and track mud everywhere. You're challenged by all sorts of outrageous adversaries, and you know it's all make believe. You learn to survive, and thrive, and win. You become powerful. You're rewarded and praised for your achievements. And when you make a bonehead mistake in a videogame, you don't get ridiculed—just encouraged to try again.

When you play with friends, video games help you to identify and belong, to earn the respect and admiration of kids who may be better athletes, or more socially polished, or can multiply six digit numbers together in their heads.

Little wonder, then, that half America's kids use a computer at home or school, and that two thirds of U.S. households with kids have a video game machine. What's surprising to many adults and shocking to some Hollywood executives is that the $7 billion video game business takes in more revenue than movie box office. Or even more than rock 'n' roll recorded music revenues.

Along with the good business has come a fair share of bad press. Part of the criticism is easy to dismiss, the part that springs from the curmudgeonliness of parents who don't like to see their kids playing with toys they've never mastered. Let's not forget that this is the first generation in which kids are playing games their dads are unable to teach them—or beat them at. So part of the resistance to video games is the threat they pose to parental control.

Other opposition to video games stems from a perception that software with martial arts or other aggressive themes may influence younger kids to accept violence as a solution to social conflict. This perception led to congressional hearings last year and proposed legislation to make game rating labels mandatory.

Every responsible independent study I've seen has concluded that kids do a spectacular job of keeping fantasy and reality in perspective.

We at Sega received our share of the criticism despite the fact that we took the initiative to have an independent board of teachers, sociologists and child psychologists review our games, so we could label them with age-rated parental advisory stickers—and we did that two years ago, one year before the issue was even raised in Washington! Most of the street fighting games were recommended for players 13 or older, and some for players 17 or older. And these games represented less than 5 percent of Sega's software library, fewer than one game in twenty.

Even if you give credence to the accusation that kids may act out video game themes in the real world—which goes contrary to every responsible study I've seen—you have to make some accommodation for the fact that kids 12 and under represent less than a third of all video game players. And adults 18 and older represent more than 40 percent of Sega's market. This comes as an astonishing statistic to many people, but it illustrates the point I made a few minutes ago, the extraordinary rapport between young people and technology.

In 1980, when Atari game machines took the consumer market by storm, players were generally 6 to 11 years old. But 1980's 11 year olds are today's 25 year olds, and they haven't lost their enthusiasm for video games. Just like adult movie goers demand more mature and complex films, adult video game players demand more mature and complex games.

Imagined disasters

Critics of video games often brush aside the demographics, arguing that mature-rated games will inevitably get into the hands of kids and will inevitably impart a tendency to act out violent behavior. That argument bothers me, and it should bother you, as well.

First, it takes a very pessimistic view of parents, that they can't or won't monitor advisory labels on their kids' video games. I, along with just about every parent I know, use the movie rating system religiously to monitor the films I let my kids see. I don't have to understand or appreciate the content of the film to make appropriate use of the MPAA rating system.

By the way, it's almost humorous the way people agonize over imagined disasters associated with each new media revolution. Historians recall that the Guttenberg press was going to corrupt the masses with unholy thoughts. The radio shows of the 20's were going to begin unraveling our moral fiber, and the movies were going to finish the job. Now television and video games are the villains. I just wish they'd hurry up with video telephony . . . give the pessimists something new to worry about.

But you know what upsets me about the attacks on video games? It's the absurdly pessimistic view those attacks take of kids—that kids can't differentiate between make-believe aggression and real aggression. That view suggests that kids passively absorb the themes in video games, rather than interpreting and learning from them.

Every responsible independent study I've seen has concluded that kids do a spectacular job of keeping fantasy and reality in perspective. The studies have also concluded that video games are played primarily for relaxation, not agitation, that they sharpen rather than dull the mind, and develop rather than retard social skills.

Studies by child psychologists such as Dr. Ernest Lotecka of Harvard and Dr. Jeffrey Goldstein of Temple University and the University of Utrecht have repeatedly assessed the impact of games on the emotions, academics, socialization and self-image of children.

Every responsible study concluded that kids easily differentiate between pretend aggressive play and real aggressive behavior.

Two little boys wrestling for fun playing out Power Rangers or playing a martial arts video game—that's pretend aggression. Two little girls excluding a third girl from a play house tea party is real aggression. Parents and educators who look casually at boys playing out fighting games are quick to condemn—because the content of the games mirrors real societal problems. But to jump to the conclusion that game content leads to really inappropriate behavior is like speculating that students studying the Napoleonic Wars may lay siege to their neighborhood.

Games improve academic performance

Ironically, this video game medium, which has received so much more than its share of media flak, has been shown by Dr. Lotecka's, Dr. Goldstein's and many other studies to make significant contributions to academic performance and socialization.

Now, why should game play improve your performance in school? The answer is obvious to every game fan—video games are designed by very smart people to be very hard to beat. A typical game takes 50 to 100 hours to play through to the end, and beating a game takes more than good eye-hand coordination. Getting past all the puzzles, obstacles, and hidden clues takes critical thinking, deductive reasoning and problem solving—key skills for academic success. What a game fan probably won't be able to tell you is that video games are ideal from an educational design perspective—they promote curiosity, personalize exploration, adjust to an individual's pace, reward all levels of achievement, instill learning patterns, and foster cooperative group participation.

How can video games build social skills? Simple, again, if you talk to game players, well over 90 percent will tell you that they prefer to play socially, which is why most of our games have provisions for two or more players. Video games, like sports, give kids a chance to break the ice and make new friends, to show their prowess and win the esteem of others.

So it shouldn't come as a surprise to learn that playing with software can do a lot for kids' self-esteem. Games let them act out the role of mythical heroes, superheroes, and sports heroes. Games let them take control of their destiny, and to get full credit for their achievements.

Two little boys . . . playing a martial arts video game—that's pretend aggression. Two little girls excluding a third girl from a play house tea party is real aggression.

All well and good, teachers and parents will say, but the problem isn't getting kids to play games, it's getting them to learn basic life skills. And they're right. The problem is that schools don't compete very successfully for kids' attention, when kids' expectations are being set by television and video games.

Imagine this: 100 years ago, when H.G. Wells first created his time machine, three people take a ride on that time machine 100 years into the future to this year—1994. A doctor, a builder, and a teacher. They each go to a place where their profession is still practiced. The doctor is absolutely bewildered by the new instruments and techniques. The builder is stunned by the power tools and new materials. But the teacher feels right at home, like nothing much has changed—same-looking room, similar desks, even some of the same books, big blackboard,—so he walks right up to the front of the classroom, picks up a piece of chalk, and starts lecturing.

Although the classroom may not have changed much, kids have. In the 1890s, I imagine they were taught to respond with polite attention when somebody lectured in front of them and drew on a blackboard. But our kids have been taught from the time they're two, if something bores you, push the button on the remote control. Zap it. Fast forward it. Change the channel. Reset the game. Load new software.

Tough crowd, that sixth grade class. Try as hard as you want, you'll never bore them into learning the capital of Switzerland. But make a game out of it, and they'll soon be fighting to see who gets the world atlas first.

Carmen San Diego

That's precisely what happened when the first Carmen San Diego was released. Kids all over the world started learning geography. Not because anyone told them they had to, or because anyone threatened them with a lifetime of burger flipping if they failed to. But because they wanted to, because learning geography was the key to beating a game that had them hooked.

Note, by the way, that Carmen San Diego wasn't designed to be educational. It was designed as a game. And, in fact, Carmen San Diego doesn't just teach. It does something more precious by far. It motivates you to learn. It motivates you because you've dedicated yourself to beating the game, you've put your self-esteem on the line, and the only way you're going to win is if you know your geography cold.

Therein lies the learning magic of a well-designed game. If the game hooks you, you'll learn facts about sub-atomic quantum physics, if that's what it takes to win.

Here's where educators and game designers can team up so effectively. Video game designers know how to create a process, a series of escalating challenges that keeps kids—and adults—engaged for 50 to 100 hours, until they succeed in overcoming the final obstacle and declaring victory. Educators know content, the substance of which knowledge is made.

Combine process and content, and you've created a learning exercise that kids will engage in voluntarily, with enthusiasm. Get it right, and you'll soon see the glowing faces of kids who associate the joy of beating the game with the acquisition of the knowledge that enabled them to win.

Sounds easy, doesn't it? In fact, it's not all that difficult, but for every Carmen San Diego, there have been dozens, maybe hundreds of pieces of educational software that kids wouldn't touch on a bet.

The problem with most educational software for personal computers— and there are a couple thousand titles—is that their developers neglected the game design side. Most educational software has pretty pictures, nice music and animation, but a game needs more than that. A game needs an alter ego for the player to occupy, a clear objective, constantly escalating challenges, more interactivity than just changing the picture or choosing an answer, and a satisfying system of escalating rewards.

So it's not too surprising that the top two or three video games outsold all the thousands of educational software combined every year for the past five years. Even with the spectacular boom in home PC sales.

In 1993, Christopher Dede, director of the Center for Interactive Technology at George Mason University, made an astonishing suggestion— that video games be used to introduce young kids to concepts like quantum mechanics, organic chemistry, and non-Euclidean geometry. Not actually teach the subjects—which are, after all, pretty much college level—but to give kids a comfort level, an intuitive sense of the way particles move, or how molecules look close up, or how there might be shapes of objects we'll never see on earth. De-mystify science when kids are young, Dede says, and you'll generate enthusiastic and capable scholars.

I have little doubt that he's right.

Because, in video games, kids strive for power. If the game is designed to deliver that power in exchange for the player's quest for knowledge, we'll have embedded a profound appreciation for the equation, knowledge equals power.

---

*Games let [children] take control of their destiny,
and to get full credit for their achievements.*

Unfortunately, the wonderful video games described by professor Dede don't exist. Nor are there enough educational games of any description for the fifty million game machines in U.S. homes. For every game on a Sega system, like Math Blaster, Carmen San Diego, and Art Alive, there are dozens of more mainstream action games. It's not that the companies who publish these games are indifferent to education. It's just that when they have to choose between the predictable development cost and profitability of an action game, and the unknown cost and sales results of an educational title, they'd be betraying their stockholders by passing up the relatively sure winner.

In fact, as described in a recent article by Alain Jehler in *Technology Review,* educational video game software is far too important a long term opportunity to leave to private companies and their unavoidable emphasis on near term results. Jehler proposes the creation of a Public Videogame Service, to fund, foster, and distribute educational software for videogame machines. He compares his proposed Public Videogame Service to PBS television, which gave birth to programs like *Sesame Street* and *The Electric Company*—shows which might not have made the cut on commercial networks.

Jehler's proposal has even more going for it if learning-rich video game software can be distributed electronically, on the information superhighway. We've all heard the promises of the "wired America." But the truth is, we're probably at least ten years away from getting even half our homes hooked into broadband networks.

The digital bike path

In the meantime, there's something already in place that I jokingly like to call the digital bike path. It's a combination of cable television and video game machines. Two thirds of U.S. homes have a game machine, and about that many have cable. A few months ago, along with our partners TimeWarner and TCI, we began testing a new cable service called the Sega Channel.

Sega Channel delivers video games into cable homes through ordinary analog cable. You don't need any fancy expensive digital set-top box at home, just a Sega Genesis and a cable adapter. The cable operator doesn't need an expensive system upgrade either, just a simple PC at the head end.

Because the technology is so basic, the value for consumers is terrific. Fifty games a month for the price of HBO or Showtime. That's $2,500 worth of video games for about $12 to $15 a month. Play any game you want, whenever you want, twenty-four hours a day, seven days a week.

So far, well over half the U.S. cable operators have agreed to offer Sega Channel. Unlike with regular video services, which occupy a big chunk of cable spectrum, Sega Channel is a thin bitstream that slips around and in between video channels. So cable operators can add Sega Channel to their mix of services without dropping any of their current channels.

Sega Channel is the first entertainment-on-demand service most American homes will see. It's also a perfect example of how prudent use of technology can deliver interactive software to the home conveniently, affordably, and quickly.

Each month, along with sports, action, and strategy games, Sega Channel will offer a library of learning games. I'm hoping many parents and many kids will discover just how much fun and how motivating these learning games can be.

While the Sega Channel can bring those games, via cable, to a wide swatch of American households and to a range of kids, our newest hardware on the market, next month in fact, is PICO, a child's first computer that is also a computer that thinks it's a toy. With PICO, kids 7 and under will have a play and learning experience with what looks like a colorful laptop PC, yet is an electronic learning aid that plugs into your TV.

All the titles for this product—called "storyware" because the software looks like a standard illustrated book for kids, yet has a computer ROM that plugs into the PICO micro-circuitry—provide fun experiences of learning and discovery centered around characters created by people like famed children's book author . . . Richard Scarry. We say this product is like broccoli to parents and ice cream to kids because it engages a child's mind in the form of interactivity and makes learning all but invisible to them.

Beyond the near term opportunities with Sega Channel, PICO, and today's game machines, I'm hoping that the entire video game community will join Sega in a serious commitment to work with educators, and that educators will reciprocate with a commitment to work with us. Together, we can create wonderful, motivating, educationally-rich software that's really fun to use, enhances self-esteem, instills a love of learning, and persuades kids that knowledge truly is power.

Thank you very much.

7

The Availability of Guns Contributes to Violent Behavior in Children

Randy M. Page and Jon Hammermeister

Randy M. Page is a contributor to the journal Adolescence. *Jon Hammermeister is an instructor in the Department of Health and Human Performance at Central Oregon Community College.*

Many studies have demonstrated that the availability of guns is responsible for the rise in violence among juveniles. These studies indicate that more than one-third of urban high school students have easy access to a gun, and many teens have access to a firearm in their own homes. Four out of every five guns brought to school come from the students' home, and handgun ownership among inner-city high school youths is closely associated with delinquent behavior. A substantial number of murders and suicides among teenagers involve firearms. Tighter gun control laws are needed to control the spread of firearm-related youth violence.

A higher incidence of weapon-carrying, and guns in particular, among youths has been identified as a key factor in the recent increase in youth violence. Weapon-carrying increases risk of death and serious injury to both the carrier and others. In recent years a number of studies have investigated the accessibility of weapons and the extent to which youth carry them.

According to the 1990 Youth Risk Behavior Survey, 1 in 20 senior high school students carried a firearm, usually a handgun, and 1 in 5 carried a weapon of some type during the 30 days preceding the survey (Centers for Disease Control, 1991). A survey of 10 inner-city high schools in four states found that 35% of male and 11% of female students reported carrying a gun (Sheley, McGee, & Wright, 1992). A study of rural school students in southeast Texas found that 6% of male students had taken guns to school, and almost 2% reported that they did so almost every day.

Reprinted from Randy M. Page and Jon Hammermeister, "Weapon-Carrying and Youth Violence," *Adolescence*, September 22, 1997, by permission of the publisher.

In addition, 42.3% of those surveyed said they could get a gun if they wanted one (Kissell, 1993). More than one-third (34%) of urban high school students in Seattle reported having easy access to handguns, while 11.4% of males and 1.5% of females reported owning a handgun. One-third of those who owned handguns reported that they had fired at someone. Further, almost 10% of female students reported a firearm homicide or suicide among family members or close friends (Callahan & Rivara, 1992). Another study from the southeast U.S. found that 9% of urban and suburban youth owned a handgun (Larson, 1994).

A poll of students in grades six through twelve conducted by Louis Harris for the Harvard School of Public Health in 1993 found that 59% said they could get a handgun if they wanted one, and 21% said they could get one within the hour. More than 60% of urban youth reported that they could get a handgun, and 58% of suburban youth also claimed that they could (Larson, 1994). Fifteen percent of students reported carrying a handgun in the past month, 11% said that they had been shot at, 9% said that they had fired a gun at someone, and 4% said they had carried a gun to school in the past year (Drevitch, 1994; Hull, 1993).

In a study of two public inner-city junior high schools in Washington, D.C., 47% of males reported having ever carried knives, and 25% reported having ever carried guns for protection or to use in case they got into a fight; 37% of females reported having carried a knife for these purposes. Both schools are located in high-crime areas (Webster, Gainer, & Champion, 1993).

Why do young people carry weapons?

A common reason given by young people for carrying weapons is for protection against being "jumped" (Price, Desmond, & Smith, 1991). However, research has shown that weapon-carrying among youth appears to be more closely associated with criminal activity, delinquency, and aggressiveness than to purely defensive behavior (Sheley, McGee, & Wright, 1992; Webster, Gainer, & Champion, 1993). Handgun ownership by inner-city high school youth has been associated with gang membership, selling drugs, interpersonal violence, being convicted of crimes, and either suspension or expulsion from school (Callahan & Rivara, 1992). Gun-carrying among junior high students is also strongly linked with indicators of serious delinquency, such as having been arrested (Webster, Gainer, & Champion, 1993). These studies have the following implications for the prevention of gun-carrying among youth (Webster, Gainer, & Champion, 1993):

If gun carrying stems largely from antisocial attitudes and behaviors rather than from purely defensive motives of otherwise nonviolent youths, interventions designed to prevent delinquency may be more effective than those that focus only on educating youths about the risks associated with carrying a gun. The latter may, however, be able to deter less hardened youths from carrying weapons in the future. Intensive and comprehensive interventions directed at high-risk children could possibly "inoculate" children against the many social factors that foster criminal deviance and the most violent behavior patterns.

How are firearms obtained? Adult criminals and youth involved in illegal activities have reported that guns are not difficult to obtain. Illegal or unregulated transactions are the primary sources of guns used in violent acts; stealing, borrowing from friends or acquaintances, and illegal purchasing of guns are the most common. Less than 1 in 5 guns used for illegal activities were purchased from licensed dealers. The most commonly cited reason for acquiring a gun is "self-defense" (Roth, 1994).

Firearms and violence

Every day in the United States there are 733 shootings (Cotton, 1992). It is estimated that 66.7 million handguns and 200 million firearms of all kinds are in circulation (Larson, 1994). About one-half of all households own at least one firearm and one-quarter own a handgun (Reiss & Roth, 1993). Experts assert that greater availability of guns increases the rates of murder and felony gun use. However, the greater availability of guns does not appear to affect levels of violence in general (Roth, 1994).

Firearm-Related Deaths Gun-related homicides, suicides, and accidental shootings account for approximately 38,000 deaths a year in the United States (Buchsbaum, 1994); approximately 60% of all homicide victims in the United States are killed with firearms. Handguns account for 80% of homicides committed with firearms, although they comprise only about one-third of all firearms owned (Roth, 1994). For the first time in many decades, the number of firearm-related deaths surpassed that of motor vehicle–related deaths in seven states (California, Louisiana, Maryland, Nevada, New York, Texas, and Virginia) and the District of Columbia (Centers for Disease Control, 1994). If recent trends continue, firearms will displace motor vehicle crashes as the leading cause of injury death nationally within a few years (Fingerhut, Jones, & Makuc, 1994). Firearm injuries primarily affect young people, resulting in greater loss of potential life years than cancer and heart disease combined.

Larson (1994) noted:

> Over the last two years firearms killed almost 70,000 Americans, more than the total of U.S. soldiers killed in the entire Vietnam War. Every year handguns alone account for 22,000 deaths. In Los Angeles County, 8,050 people were killed or wounded in 1991, according to a report in the *Los Angeles Times*—thirteen times the number of U.S. forces killed in the Persian Gulf War. Every day, the handguns of America kill sixty-four people: twenty-five of the dead are victims of homicide; most of the rest shoot themselves. Handguns are used to terrorize countless others; over the next twenty-four hours, handgun-wielding assailants will rape 33 women, rob 575 people, and assault another 1,116.

Firearms and Health Care Costs Each year, firearm attacks injure 70,000 victims in the United States, some of whom are left permanently disabled. The cost of firearm shootings, through violent attacks, accidents, or intentional self-infliction, is estimated at $19 billion nationwide for medical care, long-term disability, and premature death (New York Academy of Medicine, 1994). The average cost per firearm fatality is $373,000, and 40% of spinal injuries in inner-city areas are the result of gunshot injuries

(Cotton, 1992). A study of one urban area hospital revealed that 86% of the costs of firearm injuries are paid by taxes (Cotton, 1992).

Firearm violence and youth

Among teenagers 15–19 years of age and young adults 20–24 years of age, 1 of every 4 deaths is by a firearm. One of every 8 deaths in children 10–14 is by a firearm. For those 15–19 there are substantial variations by race and sex in the percentage of deaths due to firearms. Among African-American teenage males, 60% of deaths result from firearm injury compared with 23% of white teenage males. Among African-American teenage females it is 22% compared with 10% of white female teenagers (Fingerhut, 1993). The number of African-American males aged 15–19 who died from gunshot wounds in 1990 was nearly five times higher than the number who died from AIDS, sickle-cell disease, and all other natural causes combined (Fingerhut, 1993; Kellerman, 1994).

A poll of students in grades six through twelve . . . found that 59% said they could get a handgun if they wanted one.

In 1990, 82% of all homicide victims aged 15–19 (91% and 77% African-American and white males, respectively) and 76% of victims aged 20–24 (87% and 71% among African-American and white males, respectively) were killed with guns. Firearm homicide for African-American males 15–19 years of age was 11 times the rate among white males, 105.3 compared with 9.7 per 100,000 population. The rate for African-American females was five times the rate for white females, 10.4 compared with 2.0 per 100,000 population (Fingerhut, 1993).

In 1990, 67.3% of all suicides among teenagers aged 15–19 were the result of firearms. Since 1985 the overall rate of suicide for teenagers by firearms increased from 6.0 to 7.5 per 100,000. The group of teenagers with the largest percent increase was African-American males; however, white male teenagers (13.5 per 100,000) had a higher firearm suicide rate in 1990 compared with African-American males (8.8 per 100,000). During this same time period, the rate of suicide not involving firearms decreased for both African-American and white males and females (Fingerhut, 1993).

Controlling the carrying of weapons in schools

Schools are grappling with the problem of protecting children and school staff from the violence surrounding them. Episodes of violence, particularly gun violence, are increasing in schools (Nordland, 1992) and violent attacks involving even elementary school children appear to be on the increase. Thus, gun violence has become a major concern for schools across the nation—a concern that is no longer limited to large cities, but extends to smaller cities and rural areas (Morganthau, 1992).

School security and law enforcement officials estimate that four of every five firearms that are carried into schools come from the students' homes; they bring one of their parents' firearms for "show and tell" with friends. Law enforcement officials also note that firearms are easily accessible by other means. They are readily borrowed from friends, bought by proxy, stolen, or even rented. On the street, guns can be purchased for as little as $25.

The following position paper of the National Association of Secondary School Principals Board on Weapons in Schools outlines the need to control weapons and offers several ways in which educators can work toward that end (Kressly, 1994):

> Whereas, students have a right to attend school without a fear of weapons' violence to themselves or others;
>
> Whereas, safe schools enhance the learning environment, necessary to quality schools, which are essential to a successful democracy;
>
> Whereas, the causes of violence are multiple: chronic poverty, the lack of jobs and role models, the disintegration of families, the loss of moral values, and a popular culture that seems to glorify violence at every turn;
>
> Whereas, a major 1993 Louis Harris poll about guns among American youth reports that 1 in 25 students takes a handgun to school in a single month, and 59% know where to get a handgun if they need one;
>
> Whereas, violence is exacerbated with the increase of weapons in our schools, resulting in some 31 deaths from guns during the 1992–93 school year; be it therefore known that the National Association of Secondary School Principals:
>
> - supports passage of the Brady Bill, which requires a waiting period and background check before legal purchase of a handgun;
>
> - urges full enforcement of the Gun-Free School Zones Act of 1990;
>
> - calls on Congress to pass the Safe Schools Act of 1993, with an amendment that will ban the purchase of a handgun and semi-automatic guns for any person under the age of 21;
>
> - urges schools to provide staff training for weapons situations arising in school, and to implement student awareness programs which challenge youths' falsely held beliefs that they are invincible;
>
> - challenges schools to implement apprehension, prevention, intervention, and counseling programs to combat possession of weapons and violent acts;
>
> - encourages school-based parent involvement programs to include violence prevention strategies that emphasize the issue of easy access to handguns;

- exhorts school districts to establish violence prevention curriculum, grades K–12, and promote articulation among levels to ensure continuity in policies and practices;

- challenges Schools of Education to add conflict resolution and violence coping skills to their teacher preparation programs.

Weapon-security measures

When weapons are carried into schools, especially guns, the potential for a violent episode is heightened and, in recent years, there have been far too many violent episodes involving weapons on school campuses that have led to tragedy (Morganthau, 1992). Preventing violence calls for school policies that provide for school environments that are free from violence for students, staff, and others on school premises (Friedlander, 1993). For some school systems this may mean providing such controls as locker searches, weapons searches, hiring police to patrol school premises, allowing students to wear only see-through backpacks, and possibly providing metal detectors upon entry. Some school systems have even created separate alternative schools for young people with a history of violent and abusive behavior. While this option is attracting attention, it is also controversial (Harrington-Lueker, 1992).

Students have a right to attend school without a fear of weapons' violence to themselves or others.

A study by the American School Board revealed that 50% of school districts conduct locker searches, 36% conduct search and seizure activities, 36% maintain security personnel in schools, 31% have gun-free school zones, and 15% have metal detectors (Natale, 1994). Approximately one-fourth of large urban school districts in the United States use metal detectors to help reduce weapon-carrying in schools (Centers for Disease Control, 1993). According to the Centers for Disease Control, these detectors may help reduce, but do not eliminate, weapon-carrying in schools and to and from schools. Students who attended schools with metal detector programs were as likely as those attending schools without metal detectors to carry weapons elsewhere, but were less likely to have carried a weapon inside the school building (7.8% versus 13.6%) or going to and from school (7.7% versus 15.2%). Decreases in school-related weapon-carrying were due to decreases in the carrying of both knives and handguns. The presence of metal detectors had no apparent effect on the prevalence of threats and physical fights inside the school, to and from school, or anywhere else (Centers for Disease Control, 1993).

Security measures and equipment are expensive; walk-through metal detectors can cost up to $10,000 each and X-ray equipment designed to detect weapons in book bags can cost as much as $17,000. Hiring security personnel is also expensive. Despite these measures, students are known to have successfully carried weapons into schools, usually by sneaking them through windows or unguarded entrances, much to the frustration of many school administrators. Some school districts are reluctant to implement new security measures, particularly metal detectors, because they fear it may open them up to lawsuits (Glazer, 1992).

The need for cooperative action

It is obvious that schools alone cannot be totally effective in controlling availability of weapons. Controlling access will require the cooperation of many individuals and institutions. The New York Academy of Medicine (1994) has proposed the following:

1. Implementing a national licensure system for firearm possession;
2. Limiting the manufacture, sale, and distribution of military-style assault weapons;
3. Increasing the tax on firearms and ammunition;
4. Tightening federal licensing requirements for gun dealers;
5. Limiting the number of guns an individual can buy;
6. Implementing a gun return program;
7. Implementing a firearm fatality and injury reporting system; and
8. Educating the public to the dangers of guns and the need for national regulation.

References

Buchsbaum, H. (1994). Guns r us. *Scholastic Update*, February 11, 18–19.

Callahan, C. M., & Rivara, F. P. (1992). Urban high school youth and handguns: A school-based survey. *Journal of the American Medical Association, 267*, 3038–3042.

Centers for Disease Control. (1991). Weapon-carrying among high school students—United States, 1990. *Morbidity and Mortality Weekly Report, 40*, 681–684.

Centers for Disease Control. (1993). Violence-related attitudes and behaviors of high school students—New York City, 1992. *Morbidity and Mortality Weekly Report, 42*, 773–777.

Centers for Disease Control. (1994). Deaths resulting from firearm- and motor vehicle-related injuries—United States, 1968–1991. *Morbidity and Mortality Weekly Report, 43*, 37–42.

Cotton, P. (1992). Gun-associated violence increasingly viewed as public health challenge. *Journal of the American Medical Association, 267*, 1171–1173.

Drevitch, G. (1994). River of blood, river of tears. *Scholastic Update*, February 11, 4–5.

Fingerhut, L.A. (1993). Firearm mortality among children, youth, and young adults 1–34 years of age, trends and current status: United States, 1985–90. *Advance Data from Vital and Health Statistics* (No. 231). Hyattsville, MD: National Center for Health Statistics.

Fingerhut, L.A., Jones, C., & Makuc, D.M. (1994). Firearm and motor vehicle injury mortality—Variations by state, race, and ethnicity: United States, 1990–1991. *Advance Data from Vital and Health Statistics* (No. 242). Hyattsville, MD: National Center for Health Statistics.

Friedlander, B.Z. (1993). We can fight violence in the schools. *Educational Digest*, May, 11–14.

Glazer, S. (1992). Violence in schools. *CQ Researcher*, September 11, 787–803.

Harrington-Lueker, D. (1992). Blown away by school violence. *American School Board Journal*, 179, 20–26.

Hull, J.D. (1993). A boy and a gun: Even in a town like Omaha, Nebraska, the young are packing weapons in a deadly battle against fear and boredom. *Time*, August 2, 21–27.

Kellerman, A.L. (1994). Annotation: Firearm-related violence—What we don't know is killing us. *American Journal of Public Health*, 84, 541–542.

Kissell, K.P. (1993). Guns on rise in rural schools. *The Morning Call*, March 21.

Kressly, J.C. (1994). Targeting potential violence before tragedy strikes. *Schools in the Middle*, February, 27–30.

Larson, E. (1994). *Lethal passage: How the travels of a single handgun expose the roots of America's gun crisis*. New York: Crown.

Morganthau, T. (1992). It's not just New York . . . Big cities, small towns: More and more guns in younger hands. *Newsweek*, March 9, 25–29.

Natale, J.A. (1994). Roots of violence. *American School Board Journal*, March, 33–40.

New York Academy of Medicine. (1994). Firearm violence and public health: Limiting the availability of guns. *Journal of the American Medical Association*, 271, 1281–1283.

Nordland, R. (1992). Deadly lessons. *Newsweek*, March 9, 22–24.

Price, J.H., Desmond, S.M., & Smith, D. (1991). Inner city adolescents' perceptions of guns—A preliminary investigation. *Journal of School Health*, 61, 255–259.

Reiss, A.J., & Roth, J.A. (1993). *Understanding and preventing violence: Panel on the understanding and control of violent behavior*. Washington, D.C.: National Academy Press.

Roth, J.A. (1994). Firearms and violence. *National Institute of Justice: Research in Brief*, February, 1–7.

Sheley, J.F., McGee, Z.T., & Wright, J.D. (1992). Gun-related violence in and around inner-city schools. *American Journal of Diseases in Children*, 146, 677–682.

Webster, D.W., Gainer, P.S., & Champion, H.R. (1993). Weapon carrying among inner-city junior high school students: Defensive behavior vs. aggressive delinquency. *American Journal of Public Health*, 83, 1604–1608.

The Availability
of Guns Does Not
Contribute to Violent
Behavior in Children

Robert W. Lee

Robert W. Lee is a contributing editor to New American *magazine, a conservative publication of the John Birch Society. He is also editor and publisher of the newsletter* Comments and Corrections, *and his articles have appeared in* American Opinion, Review of the News, *and* Family Protection Scoreboard.

Guns are unfairly blamed for escalating juvenile violence. Gun control advocates concentrate only on the negative incidents involving firearms, and mistakenly believe that children who use guns for any purpose other than supervised hunting or target shooting are courting disaster. There are many more occasions of responsible firearms use than gun control supporters are willing to admit, and in many instances, children have used weapons to prevent crimes.

Advocates of gun control are inclined to portray firearms in the worst possible light while ignoring the positive aspects of gun ownership and use. They will, for example, focus on the million or so violent gun incidents committed by offenders annually, while disregarding the estimated 2.5 million-plus successful defensive uses of firearms each year. Such self-serving bias is equivalent to condemning prescription drugs because tens of thousands of persons die each year from adverse drug reactions, while ignoring the more numerous instances in which such drugs save lives.

The tendency to ignore evidence that challenges planks of the anti-gun agenda has surfaced in the wake of [the] shooting incidents at schools in Arkansas, Kentucky, and Mississippi. The major media and gun

Reprinted from Robert W. Lee, "Good Kids with Guns," *The New American*, May 25, 1998, with permission.

control zealots have sought, for example, to create the impression that when minors use guns other than for supervised hunting or target shooting, the results are inevitably disastrous. That misleading assumption was also evident in a 1994 public service advertisement (PSA) about children and guns run on several television stations in Utah. It featured the president of the Utah Chiefs of Police Association asking rhetorically, "When do you think a child, or teenager, should have a gun?" and sternly warning that "the only reason for a child to have a gun is a dangerous one."

Safety measure

But a few days before the PSA appeared, the *Salt Lake Tribune* reported an incident in Tulsa, Oklahoma in which 13-year-old Jarrod Barnes, who had been properly trained in the use of firearms, probably saved his own life and those of three younger brothers who sought refuge in a bedroom after an intruder burst into their home while their parents were away. According to the *Tribune*, while a brother dialed 911 the interloper tried to force the bedroom door open, at which point Jarrod "went for his stepfather's .357 magnum and fired through the bedroom door, striking the man in the chest." The man "stumbled into the front yard and collapsed dead." A pocket knife and 15-inch screwdriver were found on the body.

The two oldest brothers had attended gun safety classes sponsored by the Oklahoma Wildlife Conservation Department. The boys' stepfather told reporters that he considered "the older boys to be experts with firearms," adding: "We taught him [Jarrod] where to aim at the door if the door rattled. He did exactly as he was instructed." He speculated that "the firearms training the boys received probably saved their lives." No charges were filed against the parents for allowing Jarrod and his brothers to have access to the gun that may have saved their lives.

Gun control zealots have sought . . . to create the impression that when minors use guns other than for supervised hunting or target shooting, the results are inevitably disastrous.

In some instances, even paintball, cap, and BB guns have been utilized by minors to protect themselves or others. In 1994, two New York teenagers were waiting to "ambush" fellow paintball war-games friends when they noticed a female jogger being attacked on a nearby path. The youths ran to the scene, firing several warning "shots" along the way, and as the attacker fled they opened fire in earnest, hitting him nearly 30 times. The paint-splotched suspect was easily apprehended by police.

That same year in Salt Lake City, a cap gun proved to be an effective crime-fighting tool in the hands of an eight-year-old after a predator molested a nine-year-old friend. The man had dragged the older boy behind a wooden fence, molested him, and then refused to release him. Hearing the child's screams for help, his young friend rushed to his aid and, according to police, alertly fired his cap gun in the air, causing the attacker to flee. The pedophile was arrested shortly thereafter.

And in 1995, 14-year-old Nathan Archuleta was at home with the flu when confronted by a burglar in the kitchen of his home in Pueblo, Colorado. The thief grabbed a kitchen knife and slashed the boy's arm. Nathan ran to his bedroom, hoping to escape the attacker, but with nowhere else to hide he grabbed his BB gun from a dresser and shot the criminal, who stopped in his tracks, shifted into reverse, and fled from the house.

Exercising the right

There have been many instances of minors employing handguns or rifles to defend themselves or loved ones from injury or death from other persons or wild animals. Here are a handful of examples, gleaned from news accounts and the monthly "The Armed Citizen" column of the National Rifle Association's *American Rifleman* magazine:

• In 1996, although her parents and a deputy sheriff were at the scene, a 15-year-old Cookeville, Tennessee teen was forced to defend herself when an abusive ex-boyfriend eluded the deputy, kicked in the door of the home in which she was hiding, and came after her while she was calling 911. She had the phone in one hand, but a Ruger .44 magnum in the other. A single fatal shot saved her from certain harm and possible death.

• In 1992, 14-year-old Clint Reynolds of Central, Alaska was awakened by noise from a scuffle between an uncle and a grizzly bear attempting to climb through the window of the family home. Young Reynolds quickly loaded his .357 magnum revolver and fired seven shots into the bear, mortally wounding the marauding animal.

• In 1992, two teenage girls were asleep at home in Bakersfield, California when two armed men kicked in the door and demanded money. As one of the men grabbed a wallet, one of the girls grabbed a handgun and opened fire, mortally wounding the other thug. His accomplice fled.

• In 1994, a father and son teamed up to thwart a burglary. Walter Bracken and son Daniel of Albuquerque, New Mexico noticed a strange truck near another family member's home. When they went to investigate, two intruders attempted to run over the father, but Daniel, armed with a .30-30 rifle, fired several shots, wounding the driver. The other man fled. Police investigators concluded that Daniel had acted properly in self-defense.

• In 1993, after the family home had been burgled several times, 17-year-old Darren Yakunovich of Kipton, Ohio stayed home from school in the hope of apprehending the burglar. The thief did indeed strike again (it was an erstwhile friend), but when he entered an upstairs room Daniel ended his crime career, at least temporarily, by holding him at gunpoint until the police arrived.

Youthful soldiers

In our nation's early years, young people often served courageously and competently in the military. One particularly important battle of the Civil War is worth noting. The Virginia Military Institute, founded in 1839, is the nation's oldest state-supported military college. Its graduates have fought in every American conflict since the Mexican War, and the service of its entire cadet corps during the 1864 Civil War battle of New Market, Virginia marks the only occasion in U.S. history in which an entire student body has fought as a unit in pitched battle. The 257 cadets included many minors, the youngest of whom was 15.

An account of the battle by Colonel William Couper, VMI's official historiographer, in *The VMI New Market Cadets* (1933) describes how on May 15, 1864 the "deadly fire of shells, grape, canister and bullets, to which the corps was subjected . . . did not cause it to retreat or even fall back temporarily." Instead, it "began, for the first time, to fire upon the enemy." At one point, when a command was given to the corps to charge, it "was obeyed, not only with alacrity, but with enthusiasm." Indeed, "So eager were the cadets to charge the enemy, 100 or 150 yards off, that it was difficult for them to find time to load and shoot their old-fashioned muzzle loading muskets."

Not all young people who wield firearms for purposes other than hunting or target shooting do so in an irresponsible manner.

The retreating Northerners were pursued until the VMI corps "was halted by the order of [Confederate Major] General [John C.] Breckinridge." This important Southern victory, Couper notes, "temporarily preserved the Shenandoah's resources for the Confederacy." Ten of the VMI cadets either died during the battle or later from wounds they received. Another 47 suffered non-fatal wounds. The Institute eventually purchased much of the battlefield, on which it erected the nation's largest Civil War memorial to honor the youthful New Market heroes.

The incidents cited above are not intended to minimize the problem of youth violence, including gun-related violence. They are simply a reminder that not all young people who wield firearms for purposes other than hunting or target shooting do so in an irresponsible manner.

Fatherlessness Contributes to Juvenile Violence

Wade F. Horn

Wade F. Horn is a clinical psychologist and an adjunct faculty member at Georgetown University's Public Policy Institute. He is also president of the National Fatherhood Initiative, an organization whose goal is to improve the lives of children by increasing the number of children growing up with committed and responsible fathers.

There is irrefutable evidence that violent, antisocial behavior in children is linked with single parenthood. A child that grows up with only one parent is not properly prepared to function in society. Fathers instill the discipline that enables children to control their more destructive impulses. Boys who grow up without a father act out their aggressive impulses, and fatherless girls often become rebellious and promiscuous. Children of single parents account for an overwhelming portion of the prison population. To reduce the current levels of juvenile violence, society must recognize how important it is for children to be raised by both a mother and a father.

In 1960, the total number of children living in fatherless families was fewer than eight million. Today, that total has risen to nearly twenty-four million. Nearly four out of ten children in America are being raised in homes without their fathers and soon it may be six out of ten. How did this happen? Why are so many of our nation's children growing up without a full-time father? It is because our culture has accepted the idea that fathers are superfluous—in other words, they are not necessary in the "modern" family. Supposedly, their contributions to the well-being of children can easily be performed by the state, which disburses welfare checks, subsidizes midnight basketball leagues, and establishes child-care facilities.

Ideas, of course, have consequences. And the consequences of this idea have been as profound as they have been disastrous. Almost 75 percent of American children living in fatherless households will experience poverty before the age of eleven, compared to only 20 percent of those

Reprinted from Wade F. Horn, "Why There Is No Substitute for Parents," *Imprimis*, June 1997, with permission from *Imprimis*, the monthly journal of Hillsdale College.

raised by two parents. Children living in homes where fathers are absent are far more likely to be expelled from or drop out of school, develop emotional or behavioral problems, commit suicide, and fall victim to child abuse or neglect. The males are also far more likely to become violent criminals. As a matter of fact, men who grew up without dads currently represent 70 percent of the prison population serving long-term sentences.

Undeniably, fathers *are* important for the well-being of children. So, too, are traditional families. They ensure the continuity of civilization by propagating the species and socializing children. Everyone seems to understand the obvious benefits of propagation, but the important role that parents play in socializing children is widely misunderstood and undervalued.

The process of socialization

Socialization can be defined as the process whereby individuals acquire the behavior, attitudes, and values that are not only regarded as desirable and appropriate by society but that have also stood the test of time and proved to be the most humane. Proper socialization requires delaying or inhibiting "impulse gratification" in order to abide by the rule of law and the rule of custom. Well-socialized children have learned, for example, not to strike out at others to get what they want; poorly socialized children have not. Well-socialized children have learned to obey the directions of legitimate authority figures like parents and teachers; poorly socialized children have not. Well-socialized children have learned to cooperate and share with others; poorly socialized children have not.

Men who grew up without dads currently represent 70 percent of the prison population serving long-term sentences.

Much of what is described as "good character" or "virtue" reflects the ability to delay or inhibit impulse gratification. When a child tells the truth , even though he knows that it will result in negative consequences, he is inhibiting the impulse to lie to avoid unpleasantness. When he shows charity to others, he is inhibiting the impulse to behave selfishly. A civil society is dependent upon virtuous citizens who have developed this capacity to delay or inhibit impulse gratification; that is, persons who can control their behavior voluntarily. Without a majority of such citizens, storekeepers would have to post armed guards in front of every display counter, women would live in constant fear of being raped by roaming bands of marauding men, and children would be left to the mercy of those who would exploit them. Fortunately, well-socialized children generally become well-socialized adults. Unfortunately, poorly socialized children generally do not. There are few statements one can make with complete certitude, but here is one: When families fail in their task to socialize children, a civil society is not possible. Herein lies the awesome responsibility of parenting.

Socialization mechanisms

Parents socialize children through two mechanisms. The first is teaching through direct instruction reinforced by a combination of rewards and punishments for acceptable and unacceptable behavior. The second is teaching by example. Of the two, the latter is the more important mechanism since most complex human behavior is acquired through observational learning. Children are much more likely to do as a parent *does* than as a parent *says*. This is why parents who lie and cheat tend to raise children who lie and cheat, despite any direct instruction to the contrary. As Benjamin Franklin once observed, the best sermon is indeed a good example.

Please note that I have not asserted that the state—or as it is euphemistically referred to these days, the "village"—is necessary for the proper socialization of children. Rather, it is parents who are necessary, and this means a mother *and* a father. There are, of course, thousands of single mothers who are doing a heroic job of parenting and beating the odds. I do not mean to denigrate their efforts. Yet there is a great deal of hard evidence to suggest that when fathers are absent, boys tend to develop poor conduct. They "act out" their aggressive impulses, sometimes quite violently, toward others. Girls also tend to act out when fathers are absent, but in a different way; they become rebellious and promiscuous.

The importance of mothers and fathers

No matter what the advocates of "gender-free parenting" may say, mothers and fathers *do* parent differently. Mothers tend to be more verbal, whereas fathers are more physical. Mothers also tend to encourage personal safety and caution, whereas fathers are more challenging when it comes to achievement, independence, and risk-taking. And mothers tend to be stronger comforting figures than fathers who are more intent upon establishing and enforcing rules governing the behavior of their children.

The fact that mothers and fathers parent differently is not to say that one group does it "right" or "better" than the other. What children need to develop good character is the combination of what mothers and fathers bring to the parenting equation. Take the fact that mothers tend to be nurturers and fathers tend to be disciplinarians. Parenting experts used to believe that families socialize children best when both parents adopt a nurturing but permissive role, demonstrating high levels of love and low levels of control. Decades of research have shown, however, that when children are reared this way they act out through chronic bad behavior. Permissiveness as a "parenting style" simply doesn't work. Boys and girls need a high level of nurturing balanced by a high level of control. Those who are reared in families that exhibit this combination are friendlier, more energetic, and better behaved. Those who are reared by single mothers, therefore, are warm and affectionate but have difficulty learning self-discipline. Conversely, those who are reared by single fathers are obedient but often plagued by anxiety and insecurity.

It has also been fashionable for those pushing for gender-free parenting to assert that the physical play of fathers has no beneficial impact on child-rearing. Many self-proclaimed child experts exhort fathers to stop playing with the kids and do more housework. Some even claim that the rough-and-tumble play of fathers teaches aggression and should be avoided. But new clinical studies reveal that the physical play of fathers actually gives children much-needed practice in regulating their emotions and behavior and helps them develop the capacity to recognize the emotional cues of others.

What children need to develop good character is the combination of what mothers and fathers bring to the parenting equation.

The point is not to force a choice between the parenting role of mothers or fathers but to suggest that they work best when they work together. This view contrasts sharply with the "two pairs of hands" argument, which holds that when it comes to parenting, two people are better than one and it makes no difference whether they are mothers or fathers. In reality it matters greatly to whom the "two pairs of hands" are attached. Kids don't need impersonal "caregivers"; they need loving moms and dads.

Fathers are also critical to the proper socialization of children because they teach by example how to keep negative impulses in check. It is through boys' observation of the way their fathers deal with frustration, anger, and sadness that they learn how men should cope with such emotions. It is also through the observation of how fathers treat mothers that boys learn how men should treat women. If fathers treat mothers with dignity and respect, then it is likely that their sons will grow up to treat women with dignity and respect. If fathers treat mothers with contempt and cruelty, then it is likely that their sons will, too. Fathers are also critical for the healthy emotional development of girls. If girls experience the love, attention, and protection of fathers, then they are likely to resist the temptations of seeking such things elsewhere—often through casual sexual relations at a very young age. Finally, fathers are important in helping children make the difficult transition to the adult world. Boys require an affirmation that they are "man enough." Girls require an affirmation that they are "worthy enough."

The consequences of fatherlessness

Given this understanding, what should we expect when fatherlessness becomes the norm? We don't need a crystal ball to find the answer. As I indicated earlier, nearly four out of every ten children are being raised absent their fathers right now. The result is that juveniles are the fastest growing segment of the criminal population in the United States. Between 1982 and 1991, the rate at which children were arrested for murder increased 93 percent; for aggravated assault, 72 percent; for rape, 24 percent; and for automobile theft, 97 percent. Although homicide rates have increased for all ages, those for teenagers have increased more rapidly than for adults.

The teen population is expected to grow by 20 percent over the next decade, and this is precisely the generation most likely to be reared without fathers. The prospect has led many sociologists, criminologists, and law enforcement agencies to conclude that shortly after the turn of the century we will see an adolescent crime wave the likes of which has never been seen before in this country. If that were not enough, we know that each and every day:

- 7,700 children become sexually active;
- 1,100 children have abortions;
- 2,500 children are born out of wedlock;
- 600 children contract syphilis or gonorrhea; and
- six children commit suicide.

Fatherlessness is not solely responsible for these tragedies, but it certainly is a major cause. Indeed, all the available evidence suggests that improving the well-being of our children—and ultimately our nation—depends upon finding ways to bring fathers back into the home. The question is: How?

The fatherhood solution

First, our culture needs to replace the idea of the superfluous father with a more compelling understanding of the critical role fathers play in the lives of their children, not just as "paychecks," but as disciplinarians, teachers, and moral guides. And fathers must be physically present in the home. They can't simply show up on the weekends or for pre-arranged "quality time." Children need to know that their fathers are literally there for them.

Fatherlessness is not solely responsible for [destructive behavior], but it certainly is a major cause.

Second, we need to convey the importance and sanctity of marriage. While most boys and girls expect that they will eventually get married and have children, they no longer believe that there needs to be a chronology to these two events. They should be taught that marriage comes first and that it is not a trial arrangement that can be abandoned whenever conflicts arise. Here's where religious and moral instruction can make a huge difference, because children need to know that marriage is far more than a state-approved contract between two parties or a box to check on an income tax return.

Third, we must make restoring the rights and responsibilities of parents a national priority. Over the past century, child rearing has increasingly come to be viewed as a public rather than a private matter. As early as 1901, the Supreme Court of Indiana upheld a compulsory education law by arrogantly declaring, "The natural rights of a parent to the custody and control of his children are subordinate to the power of the state." The assault on parental authority gradually extended to all other areas of life. By 1960, one social worker writing in the prestigious professional journal, *Child Welfare*, felt free to note that "day care can offer something valuable to children *because* they are separated from their parents." [Emphasis added.] School-based condom distribution, "witch hunts" against parents suspected of abuse without sufficient cause, abortion on demand without parental consent—these are all contemporary examples of how the state has chosen to wage war against parents and convince children that the very people they count on most in this world are out to hurt them. In essence, the state is saying to today's children, "Do not trust your parents—we don't."

The tide is turning, however. Even many die-hard critics of the traditional family have finally been forced to admit that their ivory tower theories are wrong; in the real world, children need to be raised by two parents. And parents need the freedom to decide what is in the best interest of their own children. Another positive development is the "pro-family movement" that has grown tremendously in the last few years. There are now dozens of national and regional organizations dedicated to championing parental initiatives. And pro-family rallies have attracted stadium-size crowds around the country.

What can you do right now in your own home and your own community? You can start by pledging, "I will be a good wife and mother," or, "I will be a good husband and father." It is a simple promise, to be sure. But it is a promise upon which a good, just, and civil society depends.

10

The Breakdown of the Family Has Caused Children to Be More Violent

Patrick F. Fagan

Patrick F. Fagan is William H.G. Fitzgerald Fellow for Family and Cultural Studies, Heritage Foundation, Washington, D.C. The Heritage Foundation is a conservative think tank that advocates limited government and traditional American values.

Broken or dysfunctional homes are the main factors in determining if a child will grow up to be violent. Without the proper parental role models, a child will grow up in an atmosphere devoid of love or empathy. The social evolution of a criminal occurs in several stages. First, he is born into a highly unstable home atmosphere. Most violent criminals were raised in dysfunctional families, in an atmosphere of drugs, crime, and domestic violence. This causes him to have trouble in school and he becomes a behavioral problem. He begins to socialize with others like him, eventually joining a gang and committing crimes such as burglary and vandalism. During stage four he begins to commit violent crimes. Finally, he gets his girlfriend pregnant and the cycle starts over. Children growing up under these influences are virtually assured of perpetuating the destructive cycle.

S ocial scientists, criminologists, and many other observers at long last are coming to recognize the connection between the breakdown of families and various social problems that have plagued American society. In the debate over welfare reform, for instance, it now is a widely accepted premise that children born into single-parent families are much more likely than those in intact families to fall into poverty and welfare dependency.

While the link between the family and chronic welfare dependency is understood much better these days, there is another link—between the

Reprinted from Patrick F. Fagan, "Disintegration of the Family Is the Real Root Cause of Violent Crime," *USA Today* magazine, May 1996, by permission of the Society for the Advancement of Education, ©1996.

family and crime—that deserves more attention. Entire communities, particularly in urban areas, are being torn apart by crime. We desperately need to uncover the real root cause of criminal behavior and learn how criminals are formed in order to be able to fight this situation.

There is a wealth of evidence in the professional literature of criminology and sociology to suggest that the breakdown of family is the real root cause of crime in the U.S. Yet, the orthodox thinking in official Washington assumes that it is caused by material conditions, such as poor employment opportunities and a shortage of adequately funded state and Federal social programs.

The Violent Crime Control and Law Enforcement Act of 1994, supported by the Clinton Administration, perfectly embodies Washington's view of crime. It provides for billions of dollars in new spending, adding 15 social programs on top of a welfare system that has cost taxpayers five trillion dollars since the War on Poverty was declared in 1965. There is no reason to suppose that increased spending and new programs will have any significant positive impact. Since 1965, welfare spending has grown 800% in real terms, while the number of major felonies per capita today is roughly three times the rate prior to 1960. As Sen. Phil Gramm (R.-Tex.) rightly observes, "If social spending stopped crime, America would be the safest country in the world."

A 1988 study . . . found that "the percentage of single-parent households with children between the ages of 12 and 20 is significantly associated with rates of violent crime and burglary."

Still, Federal bureaucrats and lawmakers persist in arguing that poverty is the primary cause of crime. In its simplest form, this contention is absurd; if it were true, there would have been more crime in the past, when more people were poorer. Moreover, in less-developed nations, the crime rates would be higher than in the U.S. History defies the assumption that deteriorating economic circumstances breed crime and improving conditions reduce it. America's crime rate actually rose during the long period of economic growth in the early 20th century. As the Great Depression set in and incomes dropped, the crime rate also fell. It went up again between 1965 and 1974, when incomes rose. Most recently, during the recession of 1982, there was a slight dip in crime, not an increase.

Washington also believes that race is the second most important cause of crime. The large disparity in crime rates between whites and blacks often is cited as proof. However, a closer look at the data shows that the real variable is not race, but family structure and all that it implies in terms of commitment and love between adults and children.

A 1988 study of 11,000 individuals found that "the percentage of single-parent households with children between the ages of 12 and 20 is significantly associated with rates of violent crime and burglary." The same study makes it clear that the popular assumption that there is an association between race and crime is false. Illegitimacy, not race, is the key factor. It is the absence of marriage and the failure to form and maintain intact families that explains the incidence of crime among whites as well as blacks.

The evolution of a criminal

There is a strong, well-documented pattern of circumstances and social evolution in the life of a future violent criminal. The pattern may be summarized in five basic stages:

Stage one: Parental neglect and abandonment of the child in early home life. When the future violent criminal is born, his father already has abandoned the mother. If his parents are married, they are likely to divorce by the third year of his life. He is raised in a neighborhood with a high concentration of single-parent families. He does not become securely attached to his mother during the critical early years. His child care frequently changes.

The adults in his life often quarrel and vent their frustrations physically. He, or a member of his family, may suffer one or more forms of abuse, including sexual. There is much harshness in his home, and he is deprived of affection.

He becomes hostile, anxious, and hyperactive. He is difficult to manage at age three and is labeled a "behavior problem." Lacking his father's presence and attention, he becomes increasingly aggressive.

Stage two: The embryonic gang becomes a place for him to belong. His behavior continues to deteriorate at a rapid rate. He satisfies his needs by exploiting others. At age five or six, he hits his mother. In first grade, his aggressive behavior causes problems for other children. He is difficult for school officials to handle.

He is rejected socially at school by "normal" children. He searches for and finds acceptance among similarly aggressive and hostile youngsters. He and his friends are slower at school. They fail at verbal tasks that demand abstract thinking and at learning social and moral concepts. His reading scores trail behind the rest of his class. He has lessening interest in school, teachers, and learning.

By now, he and his friends have low educational and life expectations for themselves. These are reinforced by teachers and family members. Poor supervision at home continues. His father, or father substitute, still is absent. His life primarily is characterized by aggressive behavior by himself and his peers and a hostile home life.

Stage three: He joins a delinquent gang. At age 11, his bad habits and attitudes are well-established. By age 15, he engages in criminal behavior. The earlier he commits his first delinquent act, the longer he will be likely to lead a life of crime.

His companions are the main source of his personal identity and his sense of belonging. Life with his delinquent friends is hidden from adults. The number of delinquent acts increases in the year before he and his friends drop out of school.

His delinquent girlfriends have poor relationships with their mothers, as well as with "normal" girls in school. A number of his peers use drugs. Many, especially the girls, run away from home or just drift away.

Stage four: He commits violent crime and the full-fledged criminal gang emerges. High violence grows in his community with the increase in the number of single-parent families. He purchases a gun, at first mainly for self-defense. He and his peers begin to use violence for exploitation. The violent young men in his delinquent peer group are arrested more than the nonviolent criminals, but most of them do not get caught at all.

Gradually, different friends specialize in different types of crime—violence or theft. Some are more versatile than others. The girls are involved in prostitution, while he and the other boys are members of criminal gangs.

Stage five: A new child—and a new generation of criminals—is born. His 16-year-old girlfriend is pregnant. He has no thought of marrying her; among his peers this simply isn't done. They stay together for awhile until the shouting and hitting start. He leaves her and does not see the baby anymore.

One or two of his criminal friends are experts in their field. Only a few members of the group to which he now belongs—career criminals—are caught. They commit hundreds of crimes per year. Most of those he and his friends commit are in their own neighborhood.

For the future violent criminal, each of these five stages is characterized by the absence of the love, affection, and dedication of his parents. The ordinary tasks of growing up are a series of perverse exercises, frustrating his needs, stunting his capacity for empathy as well as his ability to belong, and increasing the risk of his becoming a twisted young adult. This experience is in stark contrast to the investment of love and dedication by two parents normally needed to make compassionate, competent adults out of their offspring.

The impact of violent crime

When one considers some of the alarming statistics that make headlines today, the future of our society appears bleak. In the mid 1980s, the chancellor of the New York City school system warned: "We are in a situation now where 12,000 of our 60,000 kindergartners have mothers who are still in their teenage years and where 40% of our students come from single-parent households."

Today, this crisis is not confined to New York; it afflicts even small, rural communities. Worse yet, the national illegitimacy rate is predicted to reach 50% within the next 12–20 years. As a result, violence in school is becoming worse. The Centers for Disease Control recently reported that more than four percent of high school students surveyed had brought a firearm at least once to school. Many of them, in fact, were regular gun carriers.

The old injunction clearly is true—violence begets violence. Violent families are producing violent youths, and violent youths are producing violent communities. The future violent criminal is likely to have witnessed numerous conflicts between his parents. He may have been physically or sexually abused. His parents, brothers, and sisters also may be criminals, and thus his family may have a disproportionate negative impact on the community. Moreover, British and American studies show that fewer than five percent of all criminals account for 50% of all criminal convictions. Over all, there has been an extraordinary increase in community violence in most major American cities.

Government agencies are powerless to make men and women marry or stay wed. They are powerless to guarantee that parents will love and care for their children. They are powerless to persuade anyone to make and keep promises. In fact, government agencies often do more harm than good by enforcing policies that undermine stable families and by misdiagnosing the real root cause of such social problems as violent crime.

The future violent criminal is likely to have witnessed numerous conflicts between his parents.

Nevertheless, ordinary Americans are not powerless. They know full well how to fight crime effectively. They do not need to survey the current social science literature to know that a family life of affection, cohesion, and parental involvement prevents delinquency. They instinctively realize that paternal and maternal affection and the father's presence in the home are among the critical elements in raising well-balanced children. They acknowledge that parents should encourage the moral development of their offspring—an act that best is accomplished within the context of religious belief and practice.

None of this is to say that fighting crime or rebuilding stable families and communities will be easy. What is easy is deciding what we must do at the outset. Begin by affirming four simple principles: First, marriage is vital. Second, parents must love and nurture their children in spiritual as well as physical ways. Third, children must be taught how to relate to and empathize with others. Finally, the backbone of strong neighborhoods and communities is friendship and cooperation among families.

These principles constitute the real root solution to the problem of violent crime. We should do everything in our power to apply them in our own lives and the life of the nation, not just for our sake, but for that of our children.

11

Violent Children Come from a Variety of Backgrounds

Maria Eftimiades, Susan Christian Goulding, Anthony Duignan-Cabrera, Don Campbell, and Jane Sims Podesta

Maria Eftimiades, Susan Christian Goulding, Anthony Duignan-Cabrera, Don Campbell, and Jane Sims Podesta are contributors to People Weekly.

Many experts point to broken homes, poverty and abuse as causes of violent behavior in children. While this is sometimes true, it is not entirely accurate. Many children who grow up in similar atmospheres do not display aggressive behavior and some violent children come from normal, indeed privileged, backgrounds. Many were raised in loving, two-parent households. Violent behavior in children cuts across all social and economic classes.

Coincidence—or scary trend? A spate of murders allegedly committed by teens leaves experts, family and police seeking answers.

During the past decade the number of murders committed by teenagers has leaped from roughly 1,000 a year to nearly 4,000. Worrisome as that trend may be, a fleeting glance at recent headlines—announcing that, in Texas, a teenage couple, formerly students at U.S. military academies, will soon stand trial for the carefully plotted murder of a girl who interrupted the smooth course of their love affair or that, in New Jersey, an 18-year-old high school senior delivered a baby while attending her prom, left the infant in the trash and returned to the dance—suggests some teens these days are also committing crimes of incomprehensible callousness. "The young people involved in some of these violent acts are without the capacity to make the connection with another life," says Dr. David Hartman, the director of neuropsychology at the Isaac Ray Center for Psychiatry and Law in Chicago. "They need have no more reason for hurting another human being than they have for peeling an orange."

How they get to that point is a matter of heated debate. Poverty, broken homes and physical, psychological and sexual abuse are frequently cited, and clearly such factors do play a role. But New York psychologist Michael Schulman, the author of *Bringing Up a Moral Child*, observes, "Given the fact that most people who suffered similar kinds of abuse don't do these kinds of things, the explanations feel a little hollow." Indeed, as the following cases illustrate, kids accused of acts of casual violence come from a variety of backgrounds. For Schulman, the solution to the problem is both straightforward and daunting. "You need to teach the child that the family stands for goodness," he says, "not simply for comfort and intellectual achievement, but that moral excellence is honored."

Kids accused of acts of casual violence come from a variety of backgrounds.

Melissa Drexler, 18 Among members of the class of '97 at Lacey Township High School in New Jersey, Melissa Drexler, 18, was known as a quiet, diligent student—an aspiring fashion designer who dreamed of becoming the next Donna Karan. She seemed shy and opened up only to a few close friends. "When you get to know her, she can be exciting," says Jim Botsacos, 18, a longtime friend. "She likes to have fun." But Drexler concealed more from her classmates than a desire to enjoy herself. Although it now appears that she was pregnant for most of her senior year, Drexler managed to hide her condition—from her classmates, parents and boyfriend, John Lewis, 20—by wearing baggy, loose-fitting clothes.

On June 6, 1997 she went to her senior prom. Dressed in a floor-length, black sleeveless velvet gown, Drexler arrived in a limousine at the Garden Manor banquet hall in Aberdeen, N.J., at about 7:45 p.m. with Lewis. She immediately retreated to the rest room with a classmate to freshen up. When her friend grew concerned that she was taking so long in one of the stalls, Drexler, Monmouth County prosecutors say, told her she was having a heavy period and to let their dates know she would be a while.

The girl returned to the rest room about 15 minutes later, and Drexler emerged, zipped her dress and touched up her makeup. A few minutes later, after asking the deejay to play a Metallica song, she hit the dance floor with Lewis, a Wal-Mart stockroom worker she had been dating for about two years. "She seemed normal," says fellow student Jeff Diab, 18. "All smiles." Meanwhile, a cleaning woman, summoned by school officials to clean up a blood-streaked stall in the ladies room, discovered the lifeless body of a 6-lb. 6-oz. baby boy in a tied garbage bag in a trash basket. After learning that Drexler was the last to use the rest room, teachers began questioning her. "She was not upset," says Monmouth County prosecutor Robert Honecker. "She indicated that she had delivered an infant." Such a blank response, though bewildering, is not unheard of, says Dr. Phillip Resnick, a professor of psychiatry at Case Western Reserve University in Cleveland. "[With] mothers who deny their pregnancy and don't form a bond, it's like a foreign body going through them—like a peach pit."

The incident has left Drexler's middle-class hometown of Forked

River in shock. By all accounts, the teenager—who could face murder charges if prosecutors can prove the baby was alive at birth—was an indulged only child whose parents, John, a computer worker, and Marie, a bank employee, provided ample love and support. But Debbie Jacobson, a classmate's mother, says Melissa "is a child emotionally. She didn't make decisions on her own about things." Adds Botsacos: "Her family is almost too nice. They didn't want her to have a job. They bought her a car, paid for her gas, bought her clothes. She got what she wanted when she wanted it." This time it seems Drexler got something she didn't want—and cast it away.

Jeremy Strohmeyer, 18 Shortly before 4 a.m. on May 25, 1997 a security camera in a Primm, Nev., casino captured 7-year-old Sherrice Iverson—on her own as her father gambled nearby—playing hide-and-seek in a video arcade with Jeremy Strohmeyer, 18, a college-bound high school senior from Long Beach, Calif. Moments later, when Sherrice dashed into the women's room, Strohmeyer followed. There, allegedly, he raped and strangled her. He then continued celebrating the Memorial Day holiday weekend with best friend David Cash Jr., 18, and Cash's father. Police say the younger Cash had trailed Strohmeyer into the rest room but left after failing to persuade him to let the little girl alone. On his return to Long Beach, a friend says, Strohmeyer told him he'd had a great time.

Little in Strohmeyer's apparently ordinary, middle-class background—his mother, Winifred, is a marketing executive; his father, John, a well-to-do real estate investor—seems to account for the callousness of the murder of which he is accused. When a Los Angeles TV station aired the surveillance tape on May 26, several stunned classmates recognized him and told their parents, who tipped off police. Two days later, Strohmeyer was arrested. (Cash, who turned himself in, was released and has not been charged in the killing.) Jean Matz, a neighbor of the Strohmeyers', was shocked. "The mother was working all the time. She is very successful," Matz says. "[John] ran the house." Once a top student and volleyball player at Woodrow Wilson High School, Strohmeyer dropped off the team two months ago and, friends say, began losing weight. His grades had plummeted. Volleyball coach John Crutchfield suspected he was using methamphetamines, but Strohmeyer denied it. Around the same time, his father threw him out of the house—for disregarding curfew, police say—though he was living at home again prior to the crime. "He would drink too much at parties to impress people," says one classmate. "Most of the time he seemed nice, but he could get obnoxious." And there was one other hint of a darker side. A friend, Andy Edling, says that earlier this year, Strohmeyer had showed him an extensive collection of pornographic photos culled from the Internet. "What struck me most was the little children," Edling says. "I thought it was gross, and he just laughed."

Daphne Abdela, 15; Christopher Vasquez, 15 For all the thousands of New Yorkers who venture into Manhattan's Central Park by day, few are aware of the hidden world that flourishes in the park after dark. That's when teenagers like 15-year-old Daphne Abdela, daughter of a millionaire businessman, come in their Tommy Hilfiger jackets and baggy pants to share the night with other would-be rebels in an odd subculture of privileged kids playing "gangstas."

On May 22, 1997 the playacting stopped; now, Abdela and her new boyfriend, Christopher Vasquez, 15, stand accused of one of the grisliest crimes in recent New York history. Police say Vasquez attacked Michael McMorrow, a 44-year-old real estate agent with whom the two had been drinking, stabbing him 30 times, almost cutting off his nose and a hand. Then, Abdela allegedly told police, she instructed Vasquez "to gut" Mc-Morrow so "it would sink" when they heaved his body into a lake.

Since their arraignment on murder charges, a portrait has emerged of two troubled teens, adrift and desperately seeking acceptance. Abdela was known as a quiet rich kid who got loud once she started drinking. "She always tried to act like she was from a bad neighborhood," says a friend. Vasquez, meanwhile, slight and bespectacled, attended the exclusive Beekman School but hoped to prove his toughness by joining a gang. A longtime friend says that in the past year, Vasquez suddenly changed. "He was never in school," he says. "He punched my friend in the face at this party . . . for no reason."

Both teens have a long history of emotional problems. Vasquez was taking Zoloft, an antidepressant, and Lorazepam, an antianxiety drug. And Abdela has undergone treatment for her drinking. Clearly her parents—Angelo, an Israeli-born top executive in an international food company, and Catherine, a French-born former model—had an inkling she was once again heading for trouble. Only one week before McMorrow's murder, they had withdrawn her from the competitive Jesuit-run Loyola School she attended and wait-listed her at the Day Top Village drug treatment center. Still, friends and teachers of both teens find the violence of the crime unfathomable. "If you're looking for some pattern of behavior," says Richard J. Soghoian, her former headmaster, "it's just not there. In fairness, it's not."

Little in [Jeremy] Strohmeyer's apparently ordinary, middle-class background . . . seems to account for the callousness of the murder of which he is accused.

Alex Baranyi, 18; David Anderson, 18   In Bellevue, Wash., a comfortable Seattle suburb, it's easy to miss the pockets of despair amid the prosperity. Yet the likes of Alex Baranyi are more common than some would admit. Baranyi, now 18, whose parents had separated when he was 8, had been taken to Pennsylvania by his father, Alex Sr., a software consultant, then sent back to Washington to live with his mother, Patricia, an educational assistant. Last November, Baranyi and his best friend, David Anderson, 18, who had left home and moved in with friends, dropped out of high school. At night they hung out with other kids at a local bowling alley and at a Denny's, where they would sit drinking coffee and killing time.

The void in their lives was filled with fantasy games. In recent years, Baranyi and Anderson had become followers of so-called goth—for gothic—subculture, in which devotees dress in black and wear white makeup to give themselves a spectral look. Baranyi was also a fan of *Highlander*, a TV series about an immortal sword-wielding hero; he owned a sword collection himself and talked often of death. "Sometimes I thought he might be sort of suicidal," says Dawn Kindschi, 17, an acquaintance who had filed a complaint against Baranyi last year after he allegedly beat her.

Despite his antisocial appearance, that was Baranyi's only serious brush with the law—until 1997. On Jan. 5 the body of Kimberly Ann Wilson, 20, was found in a Bellevue park. She had been clubbed with a baseball bat and strangled. When police went to the Wilson home to deliver the news, they found Kim's parents, William, 52, and Rose, 46, and her sister Julia, 17, bludgeoned and stabbed to death.

Lack of respect for human life cuts across all economic classes.

Acting on a tip, police brought Baranyi in for questioning. He allegedly confessed to murdering Kim, a friend of Anderson's, then to killing her family in the belief they might have known she was meeting them. Later, authorities arrested Anderson as a partner in the crime. The choice of Kim Wilson as victim may have been arbitrary. Police say Baranyi told them he simply wanted to kill someone because he was "in a rut." According to King county prosecutor Norm Maleng, evidence suggests that Baranyi and Anderson, who will go on trial in October, had committed the murders "for the sheer experience of killing." To Kevin Wulff, principal at Bellevue High, the local outcry over the slayings is a case of too little, too late. "We ignore [these kids] and hope they go away," says Wulff, "and then we are horrified when they commit these crimes."

Corey Arthur, 19 Kids like Corey Arthur were the reason Jonathan Levin got into teaching, so the irony was heartbreaking when New York City police arrested him for Levin's murder on June 7, 1997. Since Levin, 31, was the son of Time Warner CEO Gerald Levin, some thought his family's wealth had played a role in his death. In fact, police say Arthur, a dropout who was often absent from Levin's English class at William H. Taft High School three years before, chose his former teacher as a victim without knowing who Levin's father was.

Raised in New York's harshest neighborhoods, Arthur, 19, barely knew his own father, who died in April. An aspiring rapper, he had, by the age of 16, been charged with heroin and cocaine possession and had been sent to a boot-camp program for young offenders. "He felt nobody cared about him," says ex-girlfriend Crystal Jacobs. "The only love he got was from people [on the street]. He would tell me, 'You got to do right.'" A friend told *The New York Times,* "He always wanted to have money, but he never wanted to get a job."

Levin had a reputation for helping students in need. According to police, he was at his modest Manhattan apartment on May 30 when Arthur phoned asking to see him. Police say Arthur and Montoun Hart, 25 (who had seven arrests on his record), went to Levin's place late that afternoon and tortured him with a knife until he revealed his PIN number; they also say Arthur killed Levin with a bullet to the head and that $800 was withdrawn from his account at a nearby ATM machine.

Police began an intensive pursuit that ended when one of Arthur's ex-girlfriends turned him in. Charged with first-degree murder, Arthur could face the death penalty.

Amy Grossberg, 18; Brian Peterson, 19 To their parents and neighbors in the suburban enclave of Wyckoff, N.J., Amy Grossberg and Brian Peterson are simply a couple of kids who got into trouble, then made a tragic mistake. Of course the "mistake" the then 18-year-old sweethearts are accused of making involved nothing less than the murder of their newborn son and the depositing of his body in a dumpster outside a Delaware motel on November 12, 1996. Nevertheless "there's enormous support for the couple," says Joyce Harper, owner of a Wyckoff toy store where Peterson often buys Beanie Babies for Grossberg.

In an apparent attempt to explain themselves nationwide, Grossberg and her parents, Sonye and Alan, appeared on ABC's *20/20* on June 6, 1997 with interviewer Barbara Walters. "I would never hurt anything or anybody, especially something that could come from me," said Amy. Her mother, an interior designer (her husband is a furniture store owner), praised Amy's "very special" relationship with Peterson, who works part-time for his parents' wholesale video sales business and sees Amy weekly. Though Amy said nothing about her pregnancy all summer while she was home, and her parents were apparently unaware of it, Sonye characterized her relationship with her daughter as very close. "She's always so giving and caring," she said of Amy, who volunteers as an art teacher for children at Wyckoff's Temple Beth Rishon. "I can't believe that people don't see that about her."

What many viewers thought they saw instead was the Grossbergs' apparent detachment from a deeply disturbing crime. While defense lawyers argue that mitigating circumstances will become clear in court, Jerry Capone, a Wilmington, Del., attorney who represents many disadvantaged clients, says he is especially alarmed by teenagers like Grossberg and Peterson. "These kids from strong family backgrounds should have the proper moral background," he says. "That really frightens me. It means this lack of respect for human life cuts across all economic classes."

Organizations to Contact

The editors have compiled the following list of organizations concerned with the issues debated in this book. The descriptions are derived from materials provided by the organizations. All have publications or information available for interested readers. The list was compiled on the date of publication of the present volume; the information provided here may change. Be aware that many organizations take several weeks or longer to respond to inquiries, so allow as much time as possible.

American Academy of Child and Adolescent Psychiatry (AACAP)
3615 Wisconsin Ave. NW, Washington, DC 20016-3007
(202) 966-7300 • fax: (202) 966-2891
website: http://www.aacap.org

AACAP is the leading national professional medical association committed to treating the 7 to 12 million American youth suffering from mental, behavioral, and developmental disorders. The organization works to promote an understanding of mental illnesses and remove the stigma associated with them, advance efforts in preventing mental illnesses, and assure proper treatment and access to services for children and adolescents. The *Journal of the American Academy of Child and Adolescent Psychiatry* is its monthly publication of scholarly research.

American Family Association (AFA)
PO Drawer 2440, Tupelo, MS 38803
(601) 844-5036 • fax: (601) 842-7798
e-mail: buddy@afa.net • website: http://www.afa.net

AFA opposes the portrayal of anything violent, immoral, profane, or vulgar on television or in the movies. It sponsors letter-writing campaigns and compiles statistics on how media violence affects society. The association's publications include reports and the monthly newsletter *AFA Journal*.

Boys Town
14100 Crawford St., Boys Town, NE 68010
(402) 498-1400
e-mail: helpkids@boystown.org • website: http://www.boystown.org

Founded in 1917, Boys Town treats abused, abandoned, neglected, handicapped, or otherwise troubled children. Its National Resource and Training Center offers workshops, training, evaluation, and consultation services to youth and family professionals nationwide. The Boys Town Press publishes books, videos, and training materials on youth and family issues. Titles include *Reactive Aggression, High Risk: Children Without a Conscience,* and *Dangerous Kids: Boys Town's Approach for Helping Caregivers Treat Aggressive and Violent Youth.*

Canadians Concerned About Violence in Entertainment (C-CAVE)
167 Glen Rd., Toronto, ON M4W 2W8 CANADA
(416) 961-0853 • fax: (416) 929-2720
e-mail: rdyson@oise.utoronto.ca

C-CAVE conducts research on the harmful effects violence in the media has on society and provides its findings to the Canadian government and public. The organization's committees research issues of violence against women and children, sports violence, and pornography. C-CAVE disseminates educational materials, including periodic news updates.

Family Research Laboratory (FRL)
University of New Hampshire
126 Horton Social Science Center, Durham, NH 03824
e-mail: mas2@christa.unh.edu • website: http://www.unh.edu/frl

Since 1975 the FRL has devoted itself primarily to understanding the causes and consequences of family violence. FRL has gained international recognition for pioneering research which has enabled social scientists to directly estimate the scope of family violence. The laboratory publishes numerous books and articles on family violence, including *The Cycle of Violence: Assertive, Aggressive, and Abusive Family Interaction* and *Physical Punishment and the Development of Aggressive and Violent Behavior: A Review*.

Mediascope
12711 Ventura Blvd., Suite 440, Studio City, CA 91604
(818) 508-2080 • fax: (808) 508-2088
e-mail: facts@mediascope.org • website: http://www.mediascope.org

Mediascope is a national, nonprofit research and public policy organization working to raise awareness about the way media affects society. Founded in 1992, it encourages responsible depictions of social and health issues in film, television, the Internet, video games, advertising, and music. Among its many publications are *The Social Effects of Electronic Interactive Games: An Annotated Bibliography*, *National Television Violence Study*, and *How Children Process Television*.

Morality in Media (MIM)
475 Riverside Dr., Suite 239, New York, NY 10115
(212) 870-3222 • fax: (212) 870-2765
e-mail: mimnyc@ix.netcom.com
website: http://www.netcom.com/~mimnyc/index.html

Established in 1962, MIM is a national, not-for-profit interfaith organization that works to combat obscenity and violence and to uphold decency standards in the media. It maintains the National Obscenity Law Center, a clearinghouse of legal materials, and conducts public information programs to involve concerned citizens. Its publications include the bimonthly *Morality in Media* newsletter and the handbook *TV: The World's Greatest Mind-Bender*.

National Crime Prevention Council (NCPC)
1700 K St. NW, 2nd Fl., Washington, DC 20006-3817
(202) 466-6272 • fax: (202) 296-1356
e-mail: tcc@ncpc.org • website: http://www.ncpc.org

NCPC provides training and technical assistance to groups and individuals interested in crime prevention. It advocates job training and recreation programs as means to reduce youth crime and violence. The council, which sponsors the Take a Bite Out of Crime campaign, publishes the book *Preventing Violence: Program Ideas and Examples*, the booklet *Violence, Youth, and a Way Out*, and the newsletter *Catalyst*, which is published ten times a year.

National Institute of Justice (NIJ)
National Criminal Justice Reference Service (NCJRS)
PO Box 6000, Rockville, MD 20849-6000
(800) 851-3420 • (301) 519-5500
e-mail: askncjrs@ncjrs.org • website: www.ncjrs.org

A component of the Office of Justice Programs of the U.S. Department of Justice, the NIJ supports research on crime, criminal behavior, and crime prevention. The National Criminal Justice Reference Service acts as a clearinghouse for criminal justice information for researchers and other interested individuals. Among the numerous reports it publishes and distributes are *Serious and Violent Juvenile Offenders, Adolescent Violence: A View from the Street,* and *Partnerships to Prevent Youth Violence.*

National Network of Violence Prevention Practitioners (NNVPP)
Education Development Center, Inc.
55 Chapel Street, Newton, MA 02458-1060
(617) 618-2380 • fax: (617) 244-3436
e-mail: NNVPP@edc.org • website: http://www.edc.org/HHD/NNVPP

The National Network of Violence Prevention Practitioners is a rapidly growing training and technical assistance organization with more than 400 members that represent education, juvenile and criminal justice, public health, and youth and community organizations. NNVPP works to prevent youth violence, strengthen families, and restore healthy communities.

National School Safety Center (NSSC)
141 Duesenberg Dr., Suite 11, Westlake Village, CA 91362
(805) 373-9977 • fax: (805) 373-9277
e-mail: info@nssc1.org • website: http://nssc1.org

The NSSC is a research organization that studies school crime and violence, including hate crimes. The center's mandate is to focus national attention on cooperative solutions to problems which disrupt the educational process. NSSC provides training, technical assistance, legal and legislative aid, and publications and films toward this cause. Its resources include the books *Set Straight on Bullies* and *Gangs in Schools: Breaking Up Is Hard to Do* and the newsletter *School Safety Update*, which is published nine times a year.

Office of Juvenile Justice and Delinquency Prevention (OJJDP)
633 Indiana Ave. NW, Washington, DC 20531
(202) 307-5911 • fax: (202) 307-2093
e-mail: askjj@ojp.usdoj.gov • website: http://ojjdp.ncjrs.org

As the primary federal agency charged with monitoring and improving the juvenile justice system, the OJJDP develops and funds programs on juvenile justice. Among its goals are the prevention and control of illegal drug use and serious crime by juveniles. Through its Juvenile Justice Clearinghouse, the OJJDP distributes fact sheets and reports such as *How Juveniles Get to Criminal Court, Gang Suppression and Intervention: Community Models,* and *Minorities and the Juvenile Justice System.*

The Oregon Social Learning Center (OSLC)
160 E. 4th Ave., Eugene, OR 97401
(541) 485-2711 • fax: (541) 485-7087
website: http://www.oslc.org

OSLC is a nonprofit, independent research center dedicated to finding ways to help children and parents as they cope with daily problems. The center is known for its successful work in designing and implementing interventions for children and parents to help encourage successful adjustment and discourage aggressive behaviors within the family, the school, and the community. OSLC has published over 400 articles in scientific journals, written over 200 chapters in textbooks about children and adolescents and their families, published 11 books, and made many films, videotapes, and audiotapes on parenting.

The Parent Project, Inc.
2848 Longhorn Street, Ontario, CA 91761
(800) 372-8886 • fax: (909) 923-7372
e-mail: training@parentproject.com
website: http://www.parentproject.com

The Parent Project is an award-winning model for school and community programs serving high-risk families. Focusing on the most destructive of adolescent behaviors, the Parent Project's training program, *A Parent's Guide to Changing Destructive Adolescent Behavior*, offers no-nonsense solutions to the serious problems parents face raising children in today's world.

Partners Against Violence Network (PAVNET) Online
(301) 504-5462
e-mail: jgladsto@nalusda.gov • website: http://www.pavnet.org

PAVNET Online is a virtual library of information about violence and youth at risk, representing data from seven different Federal agencies. Its programs promote the prevention of youth violence through education as well as through sports and recreation. Among PAVNET's curriculum publications are *Creative Conflict Solving for Kids* and *Escalating Violence: The Impact of Peers*. The monthly *PAVNET Online* newsletter is also available.

Bibliography

Books

Janet Bode and Stanley Mack	*Hard Time: A Real Life Look at Juvenile Crime and Violence.* New York: Delacorte, 1996.
Sissela Bok	*Mayhem: Violence as Public Entertainment.* Reading, MA: Perseus, 1998.
Vic Cox	*Guns, Violence, and Teens.* Springfield, NJ: Enslow, 1997.
Kathleen J. Edgar	*Everything You Need to Know About Media Violence.* New York: Rosen, 1998.
Charles Patrick Ewing	*Kids Who Kill.* New York: Avon, 1995.
Irving B. Harris	*Children in Jeopardy: Can We Break the Cycle of Poverty?* New Haven, CT: Yale University Press, 1996.
George W. Holden, Robert Geffner, and Ernest J. Jouriles	*Children Exposed to Marital Violence: Theory, Research, and Applied Issues.* Washington, DC: American Psychological Association, 1998.
Mike A. Males	*The Scapegoat Generation: America's War on Adolescents.* Monroe, ME: Common Courage, 1996.
Dona Schneider	*American Childhood: Risks and Realities.* Piscataway, NJ: Rutgers University Press, 1995.
Victoria Sherrow	*Violence and the Media: The Question of Cause and Effect.* Brookfield, CT: Millbrook, 1996.
Sharon Stephens	*Children and the Politics of Culture.* Princeton, NJ: Princeton University Press, 1996.
Martha B. Straus, ed.	*Violence in the Lives of Adolescents.* New York: W.W. Norton, 1994.

Periodicals

William Ayers	"The Criminalization of Youth," *Rethinking Schools,* Winter 1997/1998.
Kris Berggren	"Resurrecting the Innocence Lost in Jonesboro," *National Catholic Reporter,* April 24, 1998. Available from the National Catholic Reporter, 115 E. Armour Blvd., Kansas City, MO 64111.
Jonah Blank	"The Kid No One Noticed," *U.S. News & World Report,* October 12, 1998.
Geoffrey Cowley	"Why Children Turn Violent," *Newsweek,* April 6, 1998.
Louis Gesualdi	"Don't Blame Mom for the Crime," *Humanist,* May/June 1998.

Danny Goldberg	"Does Rock Wreck Families?" *New Perspectives Quarterly*, Spring 1995.
David Grossman	"Trained to Kill," *Christianity Today*, August 10, 1998.
L. Gregory Jones	"Roots of Violence," *Christian Century*, July 15, 1998.
Gene Koretz	"Why Juvenile Crime Exploded," *Business Week*, November 24, 1997.
Richard Lacayo	"Toward the Root of Evil," *Time*, April 6, 1998.
Robert W. Lee	"Kids, Guns, and Marilyn Manson," *New American*, July 20, 1998. Available from American Opinion, 770 Westhill Blvd., Appleton, WI 54914.
Sasha Nemecek	"Forestalling Violence," *Scientific American*, September 1998.
Merri Rosenberg	"Up in Arms," *Scholastic Update* (teachers' edition), November 2, 1998.
Susan C. Vaughan	"What Makes Children Kill?" *Harper's Bazaar*, September 1998.
Robert L. Woodson	"Reclaiming the Lives of Young People," *USA Today*, September 1997.
Mortimer B. Zuckerman	"Forrest Gump vs. Ice-T," *U.S. News & World Report*, July 24, 1995.

Index